**Southern Literary Studies**

Southern Literary Studies
Louis D. Rubin, Jr., Editor

*Death by
Melancholy*

# Death by Melancholy

Essays on Modern Southern Fiction

**Walter Sullivan**

Louisiana State University Press/Baton Rouge

ISBN 0–8071–0236–9
Library of Congress Catalog Card Number 72–79339
Copyright © 1972 by Louisiana State University Press
All rights reserved
Manufactured in the United States of America
Printed by The TJM Corporation, Baton Rouge, Louisiana
Designed by Albert Crochet
1974 printing

Some of the essays in this volume appeared in the following pub-
lications: *Hollins Critic, Southern Review,* and *Southern Literary
Journal.* "Southern Novelists and the Civil War" is from *Southern
Renascence: The Literature of the Modern South,* edited by Louis D.
Rubin, Jr., and Robert D. Jacobs, copyright © 1953 by the Johns
Hopkins Press. "The New Faustus: Southern Renascence and the
Joycean Aesthetic" is from *Southern Fiction Today: Renascence and
Beyond,* edited by George Core, copyright © 1969 by the University
of Georgia Press.

For Pam, Larry, and John

# Preface

.

The essays offered in this collection were written during the last few years with one exception. "Southern Novelists and the Civil War" was first published in 1953, and though it has been extensively revised in an effort to make it consonant in style and tone with the pieces that surround it, it remains a survivor from another time when my own hopes for the world and the art it might produce were more sanguine. As for the other pieces, they derive from a gloomier state of mind, but one that I must be careful not to delineate too darkly.

It is true that I believe the southern renascence to be over. With the exception of Flannery O'Connor, whose case is very special, I have read no contemporary southern writers who are worthy of comparison with those of the generation that flowered before World War II; and I am distressed by the number of critics who are caught up in what Jacques Maritain calls *chronolotry*—the worship of whatever is most recently created because it is new. I suspect further that southern literature has declined because southern society more and more participates in the spiritual malaise that appears to be overwhelming all of western civilization. We suffer from a secular gnosticism—I am obviously echoing Eric Voegelin here—that all but smothers man's inherent yearning for the transcendent and renders him blind to the true cause of the agonies and loneliness that he endures. One might start with our apparently endless war, which rages anew as I write these lines, and from there make a list pages long of the intolerable social and political faults that plague us. But these are only symptoms of a deeper sickness, which is our separation from our proper source of being.

I do not mean to say that our case is hopeless. Within the larger ambiance of our spiritual deprivation, the South has retained something of its separate identity and in weakened form some of the conditions that helped to produce the literary renascence. Good manners remain and a love of the land and an innate sense of mystery. But the old strength, the vitality that was inherent in the homogeneous culture is gone, and I see no immediate hope for its restoration.

With very much of what I say above and in the essays that follow, Louis Rubin disagrees. It is characteristic of his charity that he should have invited me to submit these dissenting documents to the series that he serves as general editor. I record this only as the most recent example of his generosity toward me through a friendship that has survived for twenty years. I should also like publicly to thank Allen Tate and George Core who read most of these essays in manuscript and who are cheerfully indefatigable in their willingness to criticize my work. There are many others who helped and guided me through the ru-

minations that issue into statements here. They are colleagues and students and priests and hunting companions
and friends both in and out of the literary profession far
too numerous to mention, and I declare my gratitude to
them all. Most profoundly, I thank my wife Jane who
cannot know how much her help has meant to me and
cannot learn how much from this small book.

Nashville
April, 1972

# Contents

*Part One*

# Allen Tate, Flem Snopes, and the Last Years of William Faulkner

Anyone who has read much of Faulkner's work is likely to remember how Ab Snopes and his son Flem came into Frenchman's Bend, bringing with them Ab's reputation as a barn burner, and how Flem, exercising a kind of quiet extortion on Jody Varner, got a job in Varner's store. Soon after, the land was filled with Snopeses. They gained control not only of the store, but of the schoolhouse and the blacksmith shop and the cotton gin; and finally Flem Snopes married Eula Varner, got the old Frenchman place for a dowry, tricked the ordinarily shrewd Ratliff into buying it at an inflated figure, and thus completed his victory over all Frenchman's Bend.

And the triumph of Snopeses in general and Flem in particular should not be minimized. Flem is a villain of sorts, a thief, a usurer, a confidence man, but more significantly, he has neither a soul nor the ordinary weaknesses of the flesh that might modify or slow his avarice. Flem Snopes in hell cheats the devil: whatever he has pledged in his Faustian compact with Lucifer either never existed or

3

has vanished, atrophied through indifference and neglect. When time comes to settle accounts, the immortal part that Flem left in Satan's keeping cannot be found. It was sealed in an asbestos matchbox, the younger devils tell their prince, and now that the moment has arrived to produce it, they find it gone. Bribe him, then, the old prince advises, since Flem insists on the letter of the trade.

But in order to be bribed, a man has to want something, and Flem's single desire is to own things for the sake of owning them, to accrue wealth not to be spent, but to be held. The full import of Flem's neutrality as a human being, the vacancy of will and appetite that surrounds his single purpose is best comprehended in the context of Faulkner's other work. Think over the list of characters that populate Yoknapatawpha—Sutpens and Sartorises, McCaslins and Compsons, Bundrens and Beauchamps, Joe Christmas and Gavin Stevens, and Dilsey and Aunt Het— all moved by pride of one sort or another, by a sense of honor or a sense of loss, by some desire to prevail, to endure, and even to make things better for themselves and for the world: against these the hollowness of Flem stands in relief. Though married to the voluptuous Eula, he has no capacity for women. The trappings of affluence, houses and conveyances and clothes and artifacts, do not tempt him. He is so apparently devoid of feeling, of sentiment or sensibilities of any sort, that his victories seem to be motivated not by self-love but by the kind of amoral instinct that prompts a snake to bite the foot that blunders near it.

In the final scene of *The Hamlet*, Flem is leaving Frenchman's Bend. He has exploited and finally exhausted his financial opportunities, and he leaves behind a citi-

zenry, almost all of whom have suffered at his hands. Mrs.
Armstid has lost the five dollars she earned weaving by
firelight. Armstid has had his leg broken and has lost his
farm. Ratliff's interest in a Jefferson restaurant has passed
to Flem, and the community at large has been affronted
by the exhibition of Ike's perversion and afflicted by the
plague of Snopes-induced wild horses that roam the countryside and upset Tull's wagon and destroy the melodeon
in Mrs. Littlejohn's boarding house. Yet the novel ends
not in tears, but in laughter, for all the agonies have been
redeemed by love.

We recall Jack Houston whose story is a compendium of
Faulkner's notions about the innocence and helplessness
of man and the undeviating and irresistible devotion of
women whose love is consummated sooner or later by the
sheer force of their mysterious wills. Houston runs away
to Texas, gets a job, takes up with a whore, and demon-
strating that curious mixture of ignorance and dark, dark
experience—think of Sutpen, Boon Hogganbeck, Ike Mc-
Caslin—turns his back on his paramour of five years,
thinking he can pay her off with no recriminations as if
she were a horse he meant to sell or a house he had rented.
He returns to Lucy Pate, who, being female, must have
known all the time that he would return, and he marries
her and she is killed. We see him at last enduring his grief
through sad twilight hours, drinking whiskey chased with
water from a cedar bucket, and challenging a fate to which
he will not bow.

The depth of Houston's bereavement proves the quality
of his love. Further, grief, all the sorrows of the heart are
a part of life, necessary to us and to what we want to become, something more than the mere price we pay for

being human. Even Mink Snopes, who shoots Houston
from ambush, loves, and is loved by his wife, and Labove,
the farm boy turned football player and law student, is
willing to sacrifice all his years of work and deprivation
for one night with Eula. And the idiot Ike loves the cow.
On the final page of *The Hamlet*, the images join. The rich
but sterile Flem leaves for Jefferson, the wife that he cannot love in the buggy beside him, the child that he did not
and could not father in her arms. Across the fence, in a
pasture of the old Frenchman place. Mrs. Armstid brings
lunch to her half-demented husband who continues to dig
for treasure that is not there. The affection and fidelity of
Mrs. Armstid through this last of a series of misfortunes
throw into relief the values that the novel has been prob-
ing and show us what a tawdry thing it is to be a Snopes.

So things stood in 1940, and so they stood with the
Snopeses for the next seventeen years. In the time that
intervened between the publication of the first and second
volumes of the trilogy, America fought and won a war,
and Faulkner, who had lived his great years in obscurity,
won the Nobel Prize; the hydrogen bomb was invented,
and the civil rights movement came to maturity, and
everywhere, including Yoknapatawpha County, the world
was changed. What I am trying to account for in this
simple recapitulation of our history is the deterioration
that set in in Faulkner's work. The society, which furnished the conditions for and the materials of his art, had
altered. Faulkner himself had grown older and perhaps
had suffered a diminution of his talent. For whatever
cause, and I shall speculate about this later, the second
book about the Snopeses is inferior to the first.

*The Town* is set in Jefferson, and in place of the more
or less omniscient author, who guided us through the bu-
colic adventures of *The Hamlet*, we have three first-person
narrators: Ratliff and the city attorney, Gavin Stevens,
and Stevens' nephew, Charles Mallison, who is still a boy.
This change in narrative technique deprives *The Town* of
some of the sweep, the large panoramic scenes that we
find in *The Hamlet*, and brings to the novel the subjec-
tivity of the limited point of view along with the complication that results from the imposition of a fictional character's judgment on the fictional events that he relates.
Although the plot of *The Town* is generally a continuation
of the story told in *The Hamlet*, the shift in environment
is deeply felt. Jefferson is not the country, and even in a
small town, land and livestock lose their significance, property tends toward abstraction, and the symbol becomes
not the farm or the horse but the bank. Our attention
moves from the palpable world of plants and animals to
considerations of social intrigue and political preference.
We need the personal views of the first-person narrators
to help us through the new conditions of the story, and
there is an inevitable change of direction. The confrontation between love and avarice, between being and nothingness, becomes a study in the ethics of possession and a
romantic statement of mortal man's stance *vis-a-vis* the
corruptible universe.

Eula as urban matron in *The Town* is no less attractive
than she was as country maid in *The Hamlet*. She remains
married to Flem, she has an affair with Manfred de Spain,
and she is loved and longed for by Gavin Stevens. But
when she offers herself to Stevens, he will not have her.
After all his sleepless nights and his days spent dream-

ing of her physical charms, he runs from her touch and
orders Eula away from him. Later in the novel, having
courted Eula's daughter Linda through her formative
years, buying her ice cream, giving her books of poetry,
he makes the same rejection of the younger and almost
as beautiful girl. Only when Eula is dead and a bas relief
of her face is affixed to her tomb do we fully understand
what Faulkner has been getting at. Eula's likeness in
stone, forever young, forever fresh, recalls for us another book and directs us once more to one of Faulkner's
favorite poems. In "The Bear," McCaslin Edmonds speaks
to Ike McCaslin.

> "But you didn't shoot when you had the gun," McCaslin
> said. "Why?" But McCaslin didn't wait, rising and cross-
> ing the room, across the pelt of the bear he had killed
> two years ago and the bigger one McCaslin had killed
> before he was born, to the bookcase beneath the mounted
> head of his first buck, and returned with the book and
> sat down again and opened it. "Listen," he said. He read
> the five stanzas aloud and closed the book on his finger
> and looked up. "All right," he said. "Listen," and read
> again, but only one stanza this time and closed the book
> and laid it on the table. "She cannot fade, though thou
> hast not thy bliss," McCaslin said: "Forever wilt thou
> love and she be fair."

The poet was talking about all the things that touch
the human heart, McCaslin says later, but we remember
the bridal couple on the Grecian urn. They will never
claim their nuptial rights, but they live and love forever
in their chastity. So it is with Gavin Stevens and Eula.
Legally, she belonged to Flem, and he uses her infidelity
at the end: fulfilling Ratliff's prediction, he spends his
knowledge of her unfaithfulness as if it were money. But
he owned her merely: being impotent, he could never en-

joy her, never possess her. Possession was for de Spain who loved her and lay with her and lost her when she died. Only Gavin was left whole; never having pursued her, he kept what he had always had: her idealized image transferred now to stone, and his unconsummated and therefore undamaged love.

This romantic notion, this turning away from the full experience of life, overshadows the history of Snopeses in *The Town* and survives to inflict a grievous flaw on *The Mansion*. The continuing story of Flem, his success as a banker, his acquisition of the de Spain house, becomes more and more tedious, and even the account of Mink's revenge is, by Faulkner's earlier standards, stilted and artificial. Mink's talk of Old Moster, his ramblings about the mortality of man are a violent distortion of his character and the apparent evasions of an artist grown tired or confused or both. For whatever the Snopeses are, they are not philosophers, not metaphysicians. In *The Hamlet* we know them by their actions; silence and cunning are their weapons; we are never allowed to get inside the mind of Flem, and the section that centers on Mink after the murder of Houston is told with objectivity and even detachment. The deterioration in style and content in *The Mansion* can be at least partially accounted for by the decline of Faulkner's moral vision.

The novel at its best delineates and embraces mankind's common fate. We know that one aspect of life is to endure suffering and bereavement; to forego that which we most desire; to stand firm against destiny that seemingly would destroy us. Thus Labove and Houston and Gavin Stevens accept the pain and win their kind of victory and in doing so tell us some of the truth about the conditions under

which we live. At the end of *The Hamlet*, the people of
Frenchman's Bend are undefeated because they have paid
the price humanity demands. So far, the vision is true, but
it remains uncompleted. Endurance, abnegation, the good
death are in themselves beautiful, but sooner or later, the
rational faculty demands an answer. We want to know
why, or to what end, and depending on our particular view
of man and his universe, we push on through the agony
toward the infinite, or we quail in the face of terror and
turn back. In the course of his career, Faulkner took both
ways, the latter to his art's great detriment.

It is here that I come to Allen Tate. I am thinking particularly of "Religion and the Old South," that essay which
remains astonishingly vital after more than forty years,
and which, in a way, is a gloss on the work of William
Faulkner. For if, as Tate proves, the failure of the southern culture was essentially a religious failure, then certainly the decline of the South's greatest novelist can be
understood in the same terms. According to Tate, the
South

> had a religious life, but it was not enough organized with
> a right mythology. In fact, their rational life was not
> powerfully united to the religious experience, as it was in
> medieval society, and they are a fine specimen of the
> tragic pitfall upon which the Western mind has always
> hovered. Not having a rational system for the defense of
> their religious attitude and its base in a feudal society,
> they elaborated no rational system whatsoever, no full
> grown philosophy; so that, when the post-bellum tempta-
> tions of the devil, who according to Milton and Aeschylus,
> is the exploiter of nature, confronted them, they had no
> defense.

Which is to say, the South had no proper theology, and
I would add, nor proper sacraments either. The culture

existed on theological and sacramental surrogates, both
of which were products of an agrarian society and therefore could not last. What passed for theology was the
fragmentary Protestant dogma undergirded by the farmer's way of looking at reality. To live on the land was to
see life whole. Citizens of the old South dealt in the concrete and comprehended the vagaries and vicissitudes of
life from their continuing struggle with the forces of nature, all of which has been said far too often for me to
dwell on it. The images of agrarian life are sacramental
in that the seasons of the year and the cycles of life speak
continually of death and resurrection. "That which thou
sowest," says Saint Paul,

> is not quickened, except it die: and that which thou sow-
> est, thou sowest not that body that shall be, but bare
> grain, it may chance of wheat, or of some other grain:
> but God giveth it a body as it hath pleased him, and to
> every seed his own body. All flesh is not the same flesh:
> but there is one kind of flesh of men, another flesh of
> beasts, another of fishes, and another of birds. . . . So also
> is the resurrection of the dead.

To be sure, the mystery observed is not the mystery
consumed, but it was enough to sustain the agrarian in his
world. But what happens when the old procedures of the
land are reduced by mechanized farming, and the woods
are destroyed by the lumber companies, and the city es-
tablishes its hegemony over the countryside? The fate of
Faulkner himself is a case in point. Throughout their not
very close acquaintance, he annoyed Allen Tate by claim-
ing to be a farmer, but clearly much of his power as a
writer was drawn from the agrarian community in which
he lived. One is tempted to say that he was ruined by
Bennet Cerf and the *New York Times* and the American

Academy of Arts and Letters, and to think that all Mal-
colm Cowley's efforts on behalf of Faulkner's work may
have been a mixed blessing for the novelist in his last
years. After the second war, after he had become famous
and rich and had begun to win prizes and appear at uni-
versities and travel for the State Department, he was
never the same. His powers had diminished and he surely
knew this. There is something particularly sad in the effort he made in *The Reivers* to recapture some of his past
glory, to rediscover the wellspring of his art. But of course,
it was not New York that did him in; it was Oxford.

The Agrarians and their sympathizers were and are forever being accused of wanting to turn back the clock, which
is curious. For who knows better the irrecoverable nature
of the past than those who feel the loss of the past most
deeply? There is no return, and it should be emphasized
that what the writer loses in an historical dislodgement is
not so much his images and his myths—he can remember
those—but the culture that supported him in his pursuit of
them. He is distracted by new fidelities, new tensions, new
alignments, and if he drew his moral conviction, which is
the foundation of his work, almost solely from the values
and usages of that civilization, then any alteration in it will
impair his gift. So it was with Faulkner. And so thoroughly
had the passing years deprived him, he turned for support
to ideology which is the death of art.

Ideology is bad for literature because it is limited by
time and space: no matter how messianic it may appear
to be or what claims it makes for the future of mankind,
it reduces itself finally to a course of, a recommendation
for, action. Thus it mires itself absolutely in the mundane
and temporal world. And of more importance, because man

is what he is, flawed morally and corruptible in nature and therefore subject to a thousand frailties of flesh and thought, ideology is always partially wrong. It can be put into practice in a civilized or even bearable fashion only when it is based on and therefore subject to the corrections of a transcendent view. The idea derives its being from the transcendent, and being is the writer's proper business. If he is true to his calling, he is existential in the ultimate meaning of that term.

Of course, Faulkner knew this, and his instincts during the years immediately following World War II were sound. He felt called upon to plunge into a discussion of the race question; but he was wise enough to make the speeches of Gavin Stevens concerning the South and Sambo and the relationship between them subordinate to the proper function of his art. *Intruder in the Dust*, for all Gavin's talk, is magnificently plotted and filled with perceptive characters. It moves with grace and energy, and it develops some of Faulkner's favorite verities: courage and dignity and the love of justice and of truth. Then came the failure of *A Fable*, a failure that Faulkner must certainly have recognized, but which, so far as I know, he never admitted to himself. There is no need to dwell on the book's deficiencies: its lifelessness, its fragmentation, the thinness of its thematic development, the drabness of its prose. The myth is never realized, but the choice of the myth was eminently right.

Faulkner's early work, as I have already suggested, had been informed and supported by a society that was Christian, though imperfectly so. Now that his culture had slipped its Christian moorings, he sought to fill the vacuum for himself. But he was in no way equipped to do so: a

knowledge of the Scriptures, a memory of sermons and
missionary societies and young people's gatherings on Sun-
day evenings were not enough. The imagery and symbolism
of *A Fable* are peculiarly obvious. We have Christ and God
the Father and St. Paul and Mary Magdalene, but they are
presented in one or two dimensions; they play roles that
are grievously oversimplified, and they give no sense of
force held in reserve. What is worse, Faulkner's view of the
Christian mythos is almost totally sentimental: which is to
say, it veers almost totally away from the mysterious in
favor of the rational; it sacrifices the transcendent for the
mundane.

This brings me once more to *The Mansion*, the last book
in the Snopes trilogy and surely the worst book Faulkner
ever wrote. A good deal of its failure can be accounted for
in terms that are strictly technical. In the first place, there
was not enough left to tell about the Snopeses, to fill another novel. All that remained unwritten of the Snopes
story was Mink's murder of Flem, and the heavy emphasis
on Linda and her relationship with Gavin pulls the book
away from its proper channel. By the time Faulkner got to
*The Mansion,* he had lost his old themes of the ethics of
possession, the destructive power of avarice, the healing
force of love. So the book must look to its plots for unity,
and they strive against each other, the various narratives
thin and self-contained. Flem, who was the prime mover
of the first two volumes of the trilogy, fades and becomes a
passive character. Gavin and Linda may still be attracted
to each other, but their love has nowhere to go and they
know it. Even Ratliff is reduced to petty political tricks
that are neither convincing nor funny.

The technical failure is a result of Faulkner's increasingly confused vision. He is, of course, right about Flem. Flem, the modern antihero, is also the eternal avaricious man. He is one of the usurers in Dante, he is Shylock and Grandfather Smallweed, and the thrust of his sterility rightly culminates in a rejection of life itself. Mink's part in this action seems to me much more dubious. I am willing to accept his desire for revenge and to suspend disbelief when, in accordance with Flem's design, he attempts to escape from prison dressed as a woman. But Mink's quest for vengeance fails to achieve the thematic priority that Faulkner claims for it.

We follow Mink in his journey from Parchman to Memphis to Jefferson, and every step is a parodic reminder of similar ways others have walked or ridden in moral significance and dramatic fulfillment: Lena Grove and Joe Christmas and the whole Bundren family, in search of a husband, in search of identity, to bury the dead. Mink journeys not to complete the marriage sacrament or to endure the sacrifice or to discharge the family obligation. Rather, he goes toward a shedding of blood that intends only to get even for past offenses, and which has no gravity or dimension beyond the paltry act itself. On the road, Mink talks of a god who is stern, but who does not play jokes, and at one point in his trip, he joins briefly a group of sectarians whose religious impulse has apparently been awakened by their experiences in the war.

Goodyhay preaches the good news of the brotherhood of men in their common suffering. His Christ is a second lieutenant, a little old for his rank, seen in a vision while Goodyhay lay wounded in a foxhole on Guadalcanal. His Eucharist consists of telling the story of how Christ, the shavetail, insisted that Goodyhay rise from the mud, pick up his friend, and walk away and never say can't, but simply to do what was required of him. Goodyhay's theology goes like this:

> Anybody that thinks all he's got to do is sit on his stern and have salvation come down on him like a cloudburst or something, dont belong in here. You got to get up on your feet and hunt it down until you can get a-hold of it and then hold it, even fighting off if you have to. And if you cant find it, then by God make it. Make a salvation He will pass and then earn the right to grab it and hold on and fight off too if you have to but anyway hold it, hell and high water be damned—

This version of the faith is at best heretical, but it does not deviate radically from the view that Faulkner always held. The best thing that he could think of to say about Dilsey, whom he admired greatly, was that she endured. And as I have already mentioned, one of the most memorable scenes in *The Hamlet* shows a grieving Houston crying out against a fate to which he will not yield. Houston's stoic defiance is supported by the last remnants of proper religious belief that persist in the culture that surrounds him. Goodyhay must make his own god and his closing prayer expresses not so much strength as defeat and weariness. "Save us, Christ. The poor sons of bitches."

But it is Linda who has no god at all, and therefore it is she who can show us the final deterioration into pure romanticism: a self-pity so profound that it encompasses the whole world. Linda is a moderately striking figure at the end of *The Town*. She has discovered that Flem is not her father, and the last time we see her in that book, she is sitting rigidly beside him at the cemetery, her white gloved fists in her lap. But then Gavin sends her to Greenwich Village, whence she emerges to fight in the Spanish Civil

War, join the Communist Party, promote integration in
Mississippi, and do man's work in a shipyard in Mobile.
Linda is a typically modern woman: she has seen too much
of evil, too much of suffering, and neither she nor Faulkner can think of any way by which this life of agony can
be made endurable except through designs for reform and
affectionate intentions. But these are not enough. They
have never been enough, and they have sufficed only when
they were pursued within the larger metaphysical context, and this context no longer prevails. Therefore, as
Flannery O'Connor has shown us in another connection, it
is perfectly logical that Linda should be driven by her sorrow over our common suffering and her love of mankind in
general to plot and help execute the murder of an individual
man. Miss O'Connor put it this way:

> One of the tendencies of our age is to use the suffering
> of children to discredit the goodness of God, and once you
> have discredited his goodness you are done with Him. . . .
> If other ages felt less, they saw more, even though they
> saw with the blind, prophetical, unsentimental eye of ac-
> ceptance, which is to say, of faith. In the absence of this
> faith now, we govern by tenderness. It is a tenderness
> which, long since cut off from the person of Christ, is
> wrapped in theory. When tenderness is detached from
> the source of tenderness, its logical outcome is terror. It
> ends in forced labor camps and the fumes of the gas
> chamber.

So Mink kills Flem, and Linda leaves Jefferson forever,
ostensibly avenged for her mother's mistreatment by Flem,
and Mink goes free for whatever time he has left with the
blessings of Gavin Stevens and V. K. Ratliff. But these two
are mere shadows of their old selves, uncertain philosophers of a new dispensation, and on the fumbling note of
their attempt to create a do-it-yourself morality, the novel

ends. To be sure, for Faulkner, and for his reputation
among us, the failure is of little consequence. His best work
is truly that—the best this country has ever had to offer,
and it is by this that we cherish him and judge him. But his
fate in his last years is the common fate of literature, not
only in the South but in other sections as well. And the
question is, how do we in the South as elsewhere build or
rebuild a world that will support us in the pursuit of all our
spiritual possibilities and therefore in our art?

I turn once more to Mr. Tate for an answer. By violence,
he says, and by a kind of violence it must be. In 1930, when
Faulkner's great years were still ahead of him and the failure of finance capitalism was an example that none could
blink at, Mr. Tate dared to dream that a radical program of
reaction to the secular society might keep us from ruin. But
his optimism for our future was not without bounds. He
wrote: "The Southerner is faced with this paradox: He
must use an instrument, which is political, and so unrealistic and pretentious that he cannot believe in it, to reestab-
lish a private, self-contained, and essentially spiritual life.
I say that he must do this; but that remains to be seen."

That we did not use our political instrument in any sort
of advantageous way is now apparent. What we did was to
try politically to save the very worst aspects of our tradition, while out of our greed and concupiscence we hastened
the demise of much that was good. And in the meantime,
Allen Tate made his separate peace. He reestablished himself in a tradition rightfully his, but more ancient than
that of the American South, and his new allegiance brought
a new profundity to his later work. Almost alone among his
contemporaries, among whom are the true geniuses of the
southern renascence, Tate's poetry has continued to de-

velop: in spite of the fragmentations and disappointments of our present time, he has discovered new levels of meaning, new usages, new forms. Think, for example, of "The Swimmers" and of "Seasons of the Soul."

What I am recommending here is what I have recommended before: that the world at large follow Mr. Tate's happy example and return directly to participation in the full metaphysical dimension of life. But I know that the direct way is not necessarily the easiest way, nor is it the road that is likely to be taken by the majority of the literate community. And although there is hope in the almost universal renewal of interest in mysticism there is an equal danger in its practice. I am thinking now of astrology and seances, of Tarot cards and Ouija boards, of religious cults, some of which are loosely based on the teachings of Christ, and of witchcraft and the Black Mass which are demonic. The human soul yearns toward mystery, but an uninformed and imprudent pursuit of the supernatural is as likely to result in evil as in good. So, for those who cannot take the immediate way, I recommend a secular intercession. The way of escape is to retrace our footsteps: not to turn back the clock, which, as I have already said, cannot be done, but to find that place where the general view was corrupted. And that was, I submit, the place where an unrestrained romanticism blinded us to the delineations of our mortal state.

What Faulkner, in his major phase, told us about life was simply the truth. He showed us that man was flawed and that out of mankind's fallen condition issued certain hurts and disappointments, perfidies and deceptions, which at best could only be partially healed, imperfectly redeemed within the earthly circumstance. Finally, when the difficul-

ties of life became too much for us, when we found that our
mere human strength and endurance were no longer sufficient to support the tragic reality, we denied reality: we
turned our backs on the truth.

All of this develops a theme that I have written about at
some length, and I do not want needlessly to repeat myself.
So let me conclude with this. Heraclitus, in the phrase made
famous by Eliot, was right. The way down and the way up
are the same. Or, as William F. Lynch puts it in his brilliant book *Christ and Apollo*, the way to the infinite is
through the finite. The way to glory is through suffering;
and our denying the basic nature of man or the principles
under which we are privileged and doomed to live as human
beings will change nothing. Our denial of the truth only
diminishes us and cheapens our art. Let us resume, then,
our efforts to tell the truth. As people and as artists, as
scholars and critics and students and citizens let us start
with the shape of a leaf, the color of a flower. But let us be
certain that we find the true shape and the true color.

For many years the world was abused by science which
told us of a truth we could not see. Our difficulty lay not in
the fact that the scientific truth did not exist. It did and
does exist. The trouble was, we were told and we believed,
that the scientific truth was the most important of all
truths and that in each of its stages it was to be viewed as
absolute finality. The scientist, looking at the maple leaf,
said, What *you* see there is unimportant. Under my micro-
scope, *I* see a truer, finer thing. But scientism is out of
fashion, now, and we have a new enemy. Those who would
build a new universe—sociologists and theologians, news-
men and politicians, and thousands of others including, I
am distressed to say, most artists and intellectuals—tell us

that our eyes deceive us. In an unhappy fulfillment of Orwell's worst predictions, our language is corrupted to the point where we are indeed told that war is peace, that peace is war, that bad is good, that hideousness is beauty. Insofar as we fail to resist these inversions, we are ourselves corrupted, and the corruption is only compounded by the fact that we are lied to and embrace lies with the best of intentions. As John Lukacs points out in *The Passing of the Modern Age*, we will not be saved from the consequences of our self-deception simply because we have abandoned truth for the sake of justice.

Therefore, I prescribe for us, for our world and particularly for our artists, a violence that Mr. Tate, writing in a more placid and realistic atmosphere could hardly have dreamed of. For only a violent shift of our vision can make us see clearly once again. Begin with the leaf and tell the truth. Begin with the flower and trust your eyes. And if we can stand the pain of seeing accurately amidst and against all the confusion of voices that tell us we are wrong, we may move from the leaf to the works of Shakespeare and from there, perhaps, to a valid, though incomplete, understanding of man himself. This does not mean we will cease to be outraged by our agonies and our cruelties to each other and our injustices, or that we will cease trying to fight against evil, but that we will stop deceiving ourselves with the belief that under some optimum social and political development, they will no longer exist.

# Flannery O'Connor,
# Sin, and Grace:
## *Everything That Rises*
## *Must Converge*

The stories in *Everything That Rises Must Converge* are
the last fruits of Flannery O'Connor's particular genius;
and though one or two of them display an uncertainty
that must have been the result of her deteriorating health,
they are for the most part successful extensions of her
earlier fiction. Godridden and violent—six of the nine end
in something like mayhem—they work their own small
counterreformation in a faithless world. Flannery O'Connor's limitations were numerous and her range was narrow: she repeated herself frequently, and she ignored an
impressively large spectrum of human experience. But
what she did well, she did with exquisite competence: her
ear for dialogue, her eye for human gestures were as good
as anybody's ever were: and her vision was as clear and
direct and as annoyingly precious as that of an Old Testa-
ment prophet or one of the more irascible Christian saints.

Her concern was solely with the vulgarities of this world
and the perfections of the other—perfections that had to
be taken on faith, for the postulations and descriptions of

them in her work are at best somewhat tawdry. She wrote of man separated from the true source of his being, lost, he thinks and often hopes, to God; and of a God Whose habits are strange beyond knowing, but Who gets His way in the end. That she was a Southerner and wrote about the South may have been a fortunate coincidence. The South furnished her the kind of flagrant images her theme and her style demanded, and southern dialogue augmented and perhaps even sharpened her wit. But the South as locale and source was quite peripheral. She once wrote Robert Fitzgerald, "I would like to go to California for about two minutes to further these researches [into the ways of the vulgar] .... Did you see that picture of Roy Rogers' horse attending a church service in Pasadena?" Had she been born in Brooklyn or Los Angeles, the surface agonies of her work would have been altered: perhaps they would have been weakened: but the essential delineations of her fiction, the mythic impulse itself would, I believe, have been essentially unchanged.

As a novelist she was not successful. She could never fill a booklength canvas: the colors thinned out, the relationships weakened, the images became, before the denouement, rigid and brittle. The weakness obviously was not in her theme, which was big enough to fill the world, powerful enough to shape some of the greatest of all literary careers in the past, and in our own time those of Eliot and Mauriac and Graham Greene and William Golding. What went wrong was technical. Flannery O'Connor used to be fond of saying that the way she wrote a story was "to follow the scent like an old hound dog." At first glance, one might conclude that her novels were written with too little forethought. *Wise Blood* is full of loose ends: the theme dribbles away through the holes in the structure. According to Fitzgerald, the idea for having Hazel Motes blind himself came to O'Connor when, stuck at the crucial point in her manuscript, she read *Oedipus* for the first time. Then the earlier parts of the novel had to be reworked to prepare for the ending.

But a lot of novels get written and rewritten this way. And some novels of real power have ends as loose as that left by Enoch Emery, who is last seen disappearing into the night in his ape's suit. Except for Haze, all the characters fade off—Hawkes and Sabbath and Hoover Shoates. The landlady fills the void in the last chapter. But what Motes means to do, and what O'Connor meant for us to understand concerning what he does, seem clear enough. Driven by the Christ he cannot escape from, the "ragged figure" who "moves from tree to tree in the back of his mind," and motions "him to turn around and come off into the dark where he was not sure of his footing," he murders his double, the false prophet of his own false religion and therefore kills that part of himself. Then by blinding himself, he exhibits the strength of belief that Hawkes was unable to muster: he redeems Hawkes's failure and turns his vision totally inward away from this world, toward the Christ who exists in the inner darkness.

A better case can be made for *The Violent Bear It Away*. The beginning is extraordinarily powerful: the old man dies at the breakfast table, the boy abandons the partially dug grave, gets drunk, and burns the house down. The lines of the conflict are clearly drawn between the scientific attitude—which is to say, the new gnosticism—of Rayber and the gift of Christian grace which Tarwater has not been able to escape. That Tarwater is a reluctant vessel enhances

the drama of the novel: he does the work of God in spite of
himself, and a part of the resolution of the story is his understanding of his role and his acceptance of it. Having
been abused by a homosexual, he has a vision of a burning
bush, and a message comes to him: GO WARN THE CHILDREN
OF GOD OF THE TERRIBLE SPEED OF MERCY. And in the final
scene he is moving toward the darkened city where the
"children of God" lie sleeping.

The characters here are fewer than in *Wise Blood*, which
is in itself a kind of virtue: every novelist needs to learn
what he can do without. The plot is rounded off neatly. The
old man has been buried by some Negroes. The feeble-
minded child has been baptized and drowned. The prophet's will has been done: Rayber is defeated. The scent has
been true and truly followed, and all ought to be well, but
the novel remains, for me at least, unsatisfactory. The difficulty does not lie in faulty concept or structure: the scenes
balance out nicely and the pace is sure. The trouble, I think,
is with the characters: brilliantly drawn and fascinating
and symbolically significant as they are, they will not hold
up through a long piece of fiction. They are too thin, in the
final analysis, and too much alike.

Yet, the characters, the clothes they wear, the gestures
they make, the lines they speak, the thoughts they think are
what make Flannery O'Connor's work so magnificently
vivid and so totally memorable. The dialogue ranges from
the outrageous to the absolutely predictable, the latter done
so well that it never fails to delight. For example, in "The
Life You Save May Be Your Own," Mr. Shiftlet says,
"There's one of these here doctors in Atlanta that's taken
a knife and cut the human heart—the human heart . . .
out of a man's chest and held it in his hand . . . and studied

it like it was a day old chicken, and lady . . . he don't know no more about it than you or me."

Or take this passage from "The Displaced Person":

> "They came from over the water," Mrs. Shortley said with a wave of her arm. "They're what is called Displaced Persons."
> "Displaced Persons," he said. "Well now, I declare. What do that mean?"
> "It means they ain't where they were born at and there's nowhere for them to go—like if you was run out of here and wouldn't nobody have you."
> "It seems like they here, though," the old man said in a reflective voice. "If they here, they somewhere."
> "Sho is," the other agreed. "They here."
> The illogic of Negro thinking always irked Mrs. Shortley.
> "They ain't where they belong to be at," she said.

Again, in "The Life You Save," Shiftlet offers the old woman a stick of chewing gum, "but she only raised her upper lip to indicate she had no teeth." In *The Violent Bear It Away*, Tarwater makes a face suitable for an idiot to fool the truant officer, the old man lies down in his coffin to try it out—his fat stomach protrudes over the top—and the wire to Rayber's hearing aid characterizes the quality of his intelligence. All this is very fine, supported as it is with O'Connor's keen sense of the world in its various aspects: the buildings and sidewalks and trolley cars of the city, the fields and trees and clouds—many clouds—and barns and houses and pigs and cows and peacocks. Her people function richly as images and often evolve into symbols.

In "A Good Man is Hard to Find," the Misfit represents the plight of man from the beginning of Christian history to the modern age, and he sets forth the dilemma with such blunt clarity that it cannot be misread. Jesus was truly

God or He was not: between being God and not being God,
there is no middle ground. If He were, then He must be followed. If He were not, then all men are free to work out
their own destinies and the terms of their own happiness
for themselves. The Misfit is aware of his own helplessness.
Life is a mystery to him: the ways of fate are inscrutable:
he denies flatly that he is a good man, and he expects
neither human charity nor the mercy of God. He knows
only that he does not know, and his awareness is the beginning of all wisdom, the first step toward faith.

It is an awareness that the grandmother and the other
characters in the story do not share. "You're a good man!"
she says to Red Sammy Butts, owner of the roadside restaurant, and he readily agrees. But he is not: nor is she a
good woman: nor are Bailey or his wife or his children
good. Their belief in their own virtue is a sign of their
moral blindness. In pride they have separated themselves
from God, putting their trust in modern technology: in
paved roads and automobiles (Red Sammy gave two men
credit because they were driving a Chrysler); in advertis-
ing messages along the highway and tap-dancing lessons
for children and in motels and pampered cats. "A Good
Man is Hard to Find" makes clear—as does *Wise Blood*—
that the characters in Flannery O'Connor's work may not
be distinguished as good or bad, or as guilty or innocent.
All are guilty, all are evil. The distinctions are between
those who know of God's mercy and those who do not, between those who think they can save themselves, either for
this life or for the next, and those who are driven, in spite
of their own failings, to do God's purpose. In the general
retreat from piety, man and the conditions under which he
lives have been perverted.

It was Flannery O'Connor's contention that the strange characters who populate her world are essentially no different from you and me. That they are drawn more extravagantly, she would admit, but she claimed that this was necessary because of our depravity: for the morally blind, the message of redemption must be writ large. This is not to say that she conceived of her art as a didactic enterprise: but rather that like all writers of all persuasions, she wrote out of her own ontological view which remained orthodox and Catholic, while the society in which she lived and for which she wrote became more profane and more heretical every day. She could no sooner have stopped writing about God than Camus cauld have ceased being an existentialist. She was committed and she had to shout to be heard.

But in writing, as in all other human endeavors, one pays his money and makes his choice. He gives up something to get something, and to get the outrageously drawn, spiritually tormented character, it is necessary to sacrifice the subtlety that long fiction demands. Complex characterization is the *sine qua non* of the novel: the characters must not only have epiphanies: they must change and develop in terms of what they have done and seen. It was the nature of Flannery O'Connor's fictional vision that discovery on the part of her people was all. When one has witnessed the flaming bush or the tongues of fire or the descending dove, the change is final and absolute, and whatever happens thereafter is anticlimax. This is why the characters in O'Connor's novels fade and become static and often bore us with their sameness before we are done with the book. But fulfilling their proper roles—that is of revelation, discovery—in the short stories, they are not boring, and they do what they were conceived to do.

In the society which is defined by the grandmother and the Misfit, the central conflict is between those who are driven by God and those who believe in their own self-sufficiency. This idea was put forth in *Wise Blood,* but the struggle took place too much inside the mind of Motes, and O'Connor's efforts at finding images for her values were not entirely successful. In the heavily ironic "Good Country People," the conflict is between two of the godless. Hulga, the Ph.D. in philosophy, is deprived of her wooden leg by Pointer, the Bible salesman, when she will not submit to his advances. But more than this, she is robbed forever of her belief in the final efficacy of the rational process. This issue is fully joined, as I indicated earlier, in *The Violent Bear It Away*: Rayber believes in the social sciences, their theories, their statistics. To him, all mysticism is superstition, nothing is finally unexplainable, and man is the product of his environment. That the latter may not be quite true is made clear from the outset by the presence of Rayber's idiot son. But Rayber sees Bishop as the kind of mistake of nature that will ultimately be eradicated in the course of scientific advancement. All things will sooner or later be subject to the control of man. Tarwater, the unwilling instrument of grace, represents the super-rational quality of the Christian impulse. Determined not to do what his uncle, the prophet, had set for him to do, he does so anyway. Every step he takes away from the task of baptising Bishop takes him closer to that very act. All his bad temper, his country cunning, and his determination to be and to act to suit himself avail no more than Rayber's educated scheming. God snatches whom He will and sets His will in motion.

One of the most successful stories in *Everything That*

*Rises*, and in my judgment one of the best pieces Flannery O'Connor ever wrote, is a shorter and somewhat more realistic reworking of *The Violent Bear It Away*. The characters in "The Lame Shall Enter First" are three: Sheppard, city recreational director and volunteer counselor at the reformatory; Norton, his son who still grieves over the death of his mother; and Rufus Johnson, a fourteen-year-old Bible-reading criminal with a clubfoot. Like Rayber, Sheppard knows the answers to everything. When he discovers, during his ministrations at the reformatory, that Rufus has an I.Q. of 140, he determines to rehabilitate him, hard nut that he is. "Where there was intelligence, anything was possible." Immediately on seeing the boy, Sheppard discovers the source of Rufus' delinquency. "The case was clear to Sheppard instantly. His mischief was compensation for the foot."

To know everything is to be able to solve everything, and therefore Sheppard sets out to rearrange life for the mutual benefit of Rufus and Norton, who, being an only child, is selfish and needs to learn to share. Reluctantly, Rufus comes to live with Sheppard, but he does nothing to make himself pleasant. Where Sheppard is kind, Rufus is surly. He betrays Sheppard's trust in many ways, the most important of which is by corrupting Norton. He disputes Sheppard's claim that when one is dead he is simply gone, that the entry into the grave is final. Rufus knows himself to be evil, and if he does not repent he will go to hell, but the good go to heaven and everybody—including Norton's mother—goes somewhere.

Sheppard points out that a belief in God or Satan is incompatible with the "space age," and in order to turn the minds of the boys from superstition to healthy reality, he installs a telescope at the attic window. Sheppard tells the boys to look at the moon : they may go there someday : they may become astronauts. But Rufus is more interested in what will happen to the soul after death, and Norton thinks what he sees in the sky is his mother. Norton kills himself in the end, preferring death to life—or rather, preferring the life to come that he has learned about from Rufus to the drab logical existence he has lived with Sheppard. The victory here belongs to Rufus, who is lame and evil and conscious of both. He takes pride in his clubfoot, not because it explains his character or causes him to be forgiven his trespasses, but because it represents to him something of the burden of being human, the lameness of soul, the weight of sinfulness that we all must endure.

In spite of its typical O'Connor grimness, "The Lame Shall Enter First" comes to a more optimistic conclusion than does *The Violent Bear It Away*. Sheppard has his epiphany. When Johnson has finally been carried off to the police station, Sheppard reflects that he has nothing to reproach himself with. "I did more for him [Johnson] than I did for my own child."

> Slowly his face drained of color. It became almost grey beneath the white halo of his hair. The sentence echoed in his mind, each syllable like a dull blow. His mouth twisted and he closed his eyes against the revelation. Norton's face rose before him, empty, forlorn, his left eye listing almost imperceptibly toward the outer rim as if it could not bear a full view of grief. His heart constricted with a repulsion for himself so clear and intense that he gasped for breath. He had stuffed his own emptiness with good works like a glutton. He had ignored his own child to feed his vision of himself. He saw the clear-eyed Devil, the sounder of hearts, leering at him from the eyes of

Johnson. His image of himself shrivelled until everything
was black before him. He sat there paralyzed, aghast.

Jacques Maritain says, in *Art and Scholasticism*, "A
reign of the heart which is not first of all a reign of truth,
a revival of Christianity which is not first of all theological,
disguises suicide as love." This is to say, in a more complex
and sophisticated fashion, that the road to hell is paved
with good intentions. And who in Flannery O'Connor's
work is without his good intentions? Only those who are
conscious of their own evil. Only those who are driven by
the grace of God. Julian, in the title story of *Everything
That Rises*, is charity itself in his view toward the world
at large; but his mother, in whose house he lives, is the ob-
ject of his scorn and hatred. He despises her for her stu-
pidity, which is real, and for her narrowness: she is
against integration. On the bus, Julian sits beside Negroes
and makes conversation with them, not because he loves
his fellow man, but to annoy his mother. Later, she pa-
tronizingly offers a penny to a little Negro boy, is knocked
down by the boy's mother, and Julian is delighted. But like
Sheppard, he, too, in the end, is forced to see his own guilt.

Once more, in the same volume, the same theme is introduced in "The Enduring Chill." The story opens with Asbury's return from New York, where he has been living
and trying to write, to his mother's farm in Georgia, where
he thinks he will die. He has come because illness has forced
him to come, and he has in his possession the only piece of
writing he was ever able successfully to finish: a long statement of his grievances, an indictment blaming his mother
for all his failures, his weaknesses, his unfulfilled desires:
he holds her accountable for every miserable thing that has
ever happened to him. The source of his present misery,

however, is his previous disobedience of one of her rules
for conduct in the dairy. Earlier he was home to do re-
search on a play he was writing about "The Negro." To get
close to his subject matter, he worked in the dairy with his
mother's hired men, and here, to prove his solidarity with
the other race, he suggested that they all drink milk together. The Negroes would not, but Asbury did, and now he
has undulant fever.

The end of "The Enduring Chill" and the end of life
as Asbury has heretofore led it are marked by the descent
of the Holy Ghost, the sign of God's mercy. But until this
point, all of Asbury's affection for mankind has been as
vague and directionless in his mind as the outlines of the
lecture on Zen Buddhism he attended in New York. Negroes for him are not human beings, but "The Negro," and
he shows kindness to those on the farm that he may learn
more about them for the advancement of his own projects.
He abhors his mother and his sister, the priest and the doctor who try to help him. But God snatches him away. Of
such is our hope.

Of the nineteen stories published by Flannery O'Connor
during her lifetime, nine end in the violent deaths of one or
more persons. Three others end in, or present near the end,
physical assaults that result in bodily injury. Of the remaining seven, one ends in arson, another in the theft of a
wooden leg, another in car theft and wife abandonment.
The other four leave their characters considerably shaken
but in reasonable case. Each of the novels contains a murder, and taken together, they portray a wide range of lesser
offenses, including sexual immorality, ordinary and otherwise, voyeurism, mummy stealing, self-mutilation, assault
with a deadly weapon, moonshining, vandalism, and police

brutality. All this, performed by characters who are for the most part neither bright nor beautiful, is the stuff of Flannery O'Connor's comic view.

Her apparent preoccupation with death and violence, her laughter at the bloated and sinful ignorance of mankind informed her continuing argument with the majority view. Believing as she did in a hereafter, she did not think, as most of us do, that death is the worst thing that can happen to a human being. I do not mean that she held life cheap, but rather that she saw it in its grandest perspective. Nor did she conceive of earthly happiness and comfort as the ends of man. The old lady in "The Comforts of Home" brings a whore into the house with her own son because she believes that nobody deserves punishment. This is the other kind of sentimental, self-serving charity, the obverse of that practiced by Sheppard and Asbury. Both kinds result from a misunderstanding of ultimate truth. But so much of even the apparent worst of O'Connor is funny, because, as Kierkegaard made clear, under the omniscience of God, the position of all men is ironic: measured against eternity, the world is but a dream.

In her work the strain of hope is strong. "Revelation" stands not necessarily as the best story she ever wrote, but as a kind of final statement, a rounding off of her fiction taken as a whole. O'Connor's version of the ship of mankind is a doctor's office and here sits Mrs. Turpin surrounded by the various types of humanity: the old and the young, the white and, briefly, the black, the educated and the uneducated, trash and aristocrat, and good country people. Mrs. Turpin's thoughts are mostly on differences, on how, if Jesus had asked her to choose, she would have come to earth as a Negro of the right sort before she would have come as a trashy white person. The conversation is of human distinctions and of the race question, and from the beginning a silent girl with a bad complexion and a Wellesley degree regards her with loathing from behind a book. Finally, while Mrs. Turpin is in the act of thanking Jesus for making her who she is and putting her where she is, the girl attacks her and calls her an old wart hog from hell.

Mrs. Turpin's satisfaction with herself is broken: for her the scuffle in the doctor's office has shaken the scheme of things: her concept of herself and her relationships with both God and man have been called into question. She has a vision at the end.

> She saw the streak as a vast swinging bridge extended upward from the earth through a field of living fire. Upon it a vast horde of souls were rumbling toward heaven. There were whole companies of white trash, clean for the first time in their lives, and bands of black niggers in white robes, and battalions of freaks and lunatics shouting and clapping and leaping like frogs. And bringing up the end of the procession was a tribe of people whom she recognized at once as those who, like herself and Claud, had always had a little of everything and the God-given wit to use it right . . . . They were marching behind the others with great dignity, accountable as they had always been for good order and common sense and respectable behavior. They alone were on key. Yet she could see by their shocked and altered faces that even their virtues were being burned away.

So no one escapes the need for grace: even the virtues of this world, being worldly, are corrupt. But it is easy to guess what Mrs. Turpin sees. Passing before her is that gallery of rogues and lunatics who are the *personae* of Flannery O'Connor's work—all of them loved from the beginning, and all of them saved now by God's mercy, terrible and sure.

# The Historical Novelist
# and the Existential Peril:
# Robert Penn Warren's
## *Band of Angels*

I want to begin my consideration of Warren as historical novelist not with *Band of Angels,* which is the subject of this essay, but with the story of Cass Mastern, which is told in the fourth chapter of *All the King's Men.* It will be remembered that Mastern, the intended subject of Jack Burden's master's thesis, was a rich young man from antebellum Mississippi. He went to Lexington to attend college, there met Duncan Trice, seduced Trice's wife Annabelle, and survived long enough to observe the vast burgeoning of his sin and to expiate his guilt through suffering. He learned that "the world is all of one piece," that actions have consequences, having observed how a series of calamitous evils followed his "single act of . . . perfidy, as the boughs from the bole and the leaves from the bough." He sought painful death and at last found it, and at his end he thought himself more fortunate than those who remained alive.

The story occupies a secondary position in the novel, but taken alone, it seems to me to be an almost perfect piece of writing. Set seventy years before the main action of *All the King's Men*, told primarily through the device of Mastern's diary, and therefore couched in the language of another era, it demonstrates a good many of the advantages that the historical perspective affords a work of fiction. The separation in time, the diction, the existence of the journal, all help to create distance between the action and the reader. Because of the method, certain passages can be effectively summarized, and the sweep of the story can be conveyed in great succinctness. It exists for us whole in stark terms of good and evil, sin and redemption, and these values are made more readily available by the gap in time. Not only are we willing to believe of the past what we cannot believe of the present—the grand action, the heroic character—but by employing attitudes and convictions of another age, Warren was able clearly to draw moral and religious distinctions that are blurred or even obliterated by our present stance.

But, of course, historical fiction, like all other kinds, has to be written. Whatever grand theme it seeks ultimately to exploit, it must begin—the writer must begin—with the concrete, with a few specific characters set in motion by a concatenation of individual acts. Then, if the people are truly realized, if they come to life and behave as we know human beings do and must behave, and if the truth of their situations is told accurately and fully and with sharp sensuous detail, the philosophy of the writer, his world view, whatever larger truth is contained in his concept of the human condition will emerge. And if he is lucky and works exceedingly well, he will perhaps say more than he knew he could say when he set out on his task of creation.

I rehearse this familiar set of principles only because

they seem to apply so aptly to the Cass Mastern story. Warren found in Cass an image that was almost perfectly designed to convey in microcosm the novel's theme of the unity of the moral fabric and the consequences of action. But we begin with Cass, who reads the Latin poets, and Annabelle, whose deep blue eyes sparkle above the candles. We see their gestures, we hear their voices speaking the words that we know they would have spoken. ("Yes, I am seven years older than you, Mr. Mastern. Does that surprise you, Mr. Mastern?") Her tears and the touch of the flesh are real, and the story is allowed to make its own way to the suicide of Duncan Trice and the accompanying broadening of image, the evolution of the private and individual guilt into the universal and public sin. Annabelle's sale of Phebe, Mastern's fight with ruffians in the house of the slave trader, the war, and Cass's death agony in an Atlanta hospital all support the final philosophical summation. "He learned that the world is like an enormous spider web and if you touch it . . . the vibration ripples to the remotest perimeter and the drowsy spider feels the tingle and . . . springs out to fling the gossamer coils about you who have touched the web. . . ." This is well put, but the humanity of Cass and Annabelle had to precede it: the simple truth of their lives, sharply delineated, had to come first. Such is the nature of all fiction, historical or not.

But Warren knows this better than most other people, and one suspects that when he came to write *Band of Angels* he must have seen in his cast of characters images fully as promising as those of Cass and Annabelle. By this time —nine years intervened between the two books—he had progressed from his original dialectic of fact and idea, the man of dreams against the man of action, to an existential

and activist orientation. He had given up completely whatever notion he had previously entertained of a created universe subject to a transcendent order. Although he remained deeply interested in the dramatic possibilities of
the past, and in certain theoretical aspects of the Civil War,
that seemed to him to bear on modern problems of race, he
had grown somewhat contemptuous of history in the larger
sense, for to the extent that life is absurd, it must always
have been that way. He had left the South and eschewed
what remained of the traditional society. All of which is to
say that he was properly alienated; his concern was with
questions of individual identity and freedom, and he had
come to have the ordinary intellectual's ordinary interest
in social justice.

So Amantha Starr must have seemed a splendid vehicle
for what he meant to do. She is deprived of identity by her
mixed blood, bound spiritually by her humanity and physically by the circumstances that make her a slave, and her
material condition symbolizes the anguish of her soul. Who
am I? she asks in the opening passage of the novel. How,
she wonders, can she be set free? Such is the overture, the
introduction of theme, and then Warren sets to work with
his customary skill. Initially, he allows Amantha her freedom; she looks at bondage from the outside, regarding its
victims with ineffectual and pompous sympathy. The first
climax of the novel comes when Amantha stands beside her
father's grave and discovers that she is legally a slave, and
that unless someone comes to her aid, she must be delivered
by the reluctant sheriff to her new owner. That no one
helps, that freedom will not come from outside, fore-
shadows the book's conclusion. But there is a good deal of
action to be got through before this epiphany is achieved.

The fact is that someone else does assist her. Hamish Bond wanders into the New Orleans auction room, defends her honor, bids her in, and takes her to his home. Bond himself is one of the lost people of the world : he is rich and self-sufficient, but he knows no better than Amantha who or what he is, and his fate, like hers, is bound up with race, although more tenuously. His name is not Bond, but Alec Hinks, and the days of his youth were filled with his mother's harangues, her lamentations for the slaves who used to serve her wants, and the gentility of the life she used to lead before she married and came to Baltimore from South Carolina. It was partly to spite his mother that Bond became a slave trader : with a sense of irony, he immersed himself in Negroes and arrived at his love-hate relationship with Rau-Ru, his dearest friend and his bitterest enemy, his alter ego, his *K'la.*

Since, in spite of the ease of his worldly circumstances, Bond is not free, he cannot offer freedom to Amantha. Or at least, the freedom that he can give her, physical emancipation, is not the freedom that she seeks. Early in their relationship, after he has yielded to the temptation to make love to her, he offers to send her north, but she remains with him until he discloses to her the story of his shameful past. Knowing at last what he has done and seen, regarding him in the light of the vast evils he has perpetrated, she, like Rau-Ru, discovers hate where she once felt affection. Now, with cotton burning on the wharfs, and Farragut waiting to capture the city, Bond turns to Amantha in bed, but these flames, this smoke remind her of the conflagrations of African villages. She feels that to be united with Bond sexually makes her a party to his guilt, one with him in responsibility for the trade he followed with all its accompanying bloodshed and agony and degradation. He forces himself on her, and thus she is released—from Bond, but not yet into freedom.

This scene, which occurs halfway through the book, marks the second distinct turn of the novel. At her father's funeral, Amantha was enslaved; now she is forever physically free. Bond has released her, but more than that, the North is winning the Civil War, the Emancipation Proclamation will soon be issued. Tobias Sears arrives apparently ready to lead her into the white world and even into the most powerful segment thereof, if only he can solve his own problems of loyalty. Sears, a New Englander and captain in the Union Army, is caught between his sense of reality, what he sees with his own eyes about the war and reconstruction, and the narrow capitalistic puritanism which is his heritage and which is exemplified by his father. Sears is the quintessential white man: Amantha insists on the paleness of his body at the moment of their marriage's consummation. But in his despair over the world and his argument with the self that he used to be, he parodies Bond in a noble way and volunteers to lead Negro troops and later works for the Freedmen's Bureau. He seeks a new identity in the cause of the black man.

We are to believe, I think, that Sears's obsession with the Negro's plight is the immediate reason, not the underlying cause of Amantha's deserting him. She has searched for a definition of herself in his whiteness, and basic to Warren's philosophy is his conviction that self-recognition comes from within, not from without. Amantha's discovery of this principle is still far off, and she turns away from white to pursue black in the company of Rau-Ru. This effort too fails, of course, but identities do begin to be found within the framework of confrontation. Rau-Ru claims black; Bond claims white; each proclaims the reality of self and chooses death in a final and absolute exercise of freedom. But Amantha is still left, and she drifts away into the Middle West with Sears, growing older in boredom and disappointment and occasional sharp grief until she and Tobias make their liberating discoveries.

Now it seems to me that the conclusion of this novel is unsatisfactory. Two Negro derelicts—one of whom remains nameless and both of whom appear only in the final pages—trigger the action. Uncle Slop is a comic figure, I suppose, though not a very original one, and he remains shadowy since we never see him directly. There is a certain effective irony in the reversal of roles: a somewhat seedy Tobias Sears is employed by the rich and black Mr. Lounberry. And what Tobias discovers is the predictable existential enlightenment. He must be himself. He must declare his own manhood. And he does so by insulting Mr. Biggers and proving thereby that he does not have to submit to the kind of persecution Mr. Lounberry has just endured.

Amantha's epiphany is a result of her believing, erroneously and against her better judgment, that an old beggar with scars on his back is Rau-Ru, escaped somehow from death in Louisiana. She gives him money she cannot afford to part with: she goes to visit his grave when he dies. There, surrounded by the sinking mounds and the parsimonious tombstones, she hears the Kansas wind whisper the truth. No one can help you. No one can set you free except yourself. Thus the questions that are raised on the first page are answered. But the conclusion does not seem to jibe with the main thrust of the book's action: the solutions do not seem to be the inevitable product of character and plot.

The failure of the ending is, in my judgment, indicative of the general failure of the novel, which is largely unredeemed by the presence of many well-conceived and fully realized scenes and some truly moving passages. Warren is a splendid prose stylist, a competent craftsman, or more than that: a thorough student of his genre, a master of technique. I need not expand on his virtues, except to say that in at least one way he is as well qualified as. any living American novelist to write about the past. He is a diligent researcher, and his eye for costume and equipment, his feel for manners, his ear for archaic patterns of speech are unsurpassed. Open *Band of Angels* anywhere, and you will find evidence of Warren's full grasp of the surface details of life as it used to be lived. Such a talent is not to be minimized: it is exactly with such minutiae that fiction begins its journey toward the truth.

But accuracies of dress and gesture are not final, and where critical argument with Warren often commences is with the ideas that burden the dialogue and inform the scenes. Are his people really believable in terms of the stern philosophical bases that start their yearnings and shape their impulses and govern their fates? Such a question, let me hasten to say, may be unfair and is certainly unchivalrous. It takes us immediately into a twilight area where the meanest sort of cavils remain largely unanswered and where judgments that are basically subjective are likely to be made. Whenever we debate the realism of characters, the verisimilitude of action, we must keep reminding ourselves that all fiction is distortion: otherwise

it would not be fiction but merely life unrefined and form-
less, a mundane record not yet vivified and made revealing
by the processes of art.

Still, fiction must convince us. Credibility is essential,
and I must confess that I find it very difficult to believe that
a teenaged girl on a plantation in antebellum Kentucky
ever really wondered who she was and what it would take
to make her free. Indeed, I doubt that very many people in
the 1850s of whatever age or sex or place of abode troubled
themselves much about the problem of identity. Existentialism as a popular philosophical stance is a manifestation
of the modern age, and to hold otherwise in a piece of fiction is to commit the most damaging sort of anachronism.
Whatever reappraisals and revisions the historians might
make, the novelist is obligated by the demands of his craft
to keep to the truth in its simplest form. That is, he must
be faithful to the spirit of the time. His characters must
share with their now dead, but once actual counterparts a
common view of life and its sources, the way it should be
lived, the ends it should serve.

We know this to be true, because in the first place, if the
study of literature discloses anything, it teaches us that
social and cultural fragmentation are bad for art. Endow-
ing characters in an historical novel with attitudes that are
not indigenous to the age is one way of creating fragmentation or exacerbating that which already exists. But this is
a lateral argument, and I shall not pursue it. More germane
is the combination of uniqueness and universality that
every author strives to achieve in the characters that he
creates. Certain writers such as Cervantes or Dickens may
lean toward the idiosyncratic, but the final ambition of
every serious novelist is to create characters so firmly

rooted in our shared humanity that each becomes a kind of
Everyman, an example of human attributes that are and
were and shall be recognizable to readers of whatever period. To succeed in this ambition is the crowning achievement of the great novelist.

But again we must remind ourselves that we proceed
from the particular; or to speak more nearly in the context of the present discussion, we must first apprehend the
individual in his specific time and place. Consider *War and
Peace*. In the opening scene of the novel, Pierre is almost
completely individualized. We are conscious of his hulking
figure, his spectacles, his uncertain manners; he is uncom-
fortable and at odds with his fellow guests at Anna Scher-
er's party. His differences stand out on this most intensely
Russian occasion. Frequently in the future he will be in
disagreement with both friends and enemies over social
and political matters. But he exists always within the limits
of historical actuality: in the particulars of his life and
thought, he never violates his own age. Because he has first
his roots in the realities of the period, he can, under Tolstoy's genius, expand as image, until, as Andrew Lytle has
pointed out, he becomes, during the occupation of Moscow,
the incarnation of his fatherland: he *is* the Russian bear.
Nor is this all. At the very end of the novel, he, along with
some of the other major figures, shows us the very sweep
of life, the repeated patterns of human generations, so that
the full implications of the book's title are made clear.

It may be argued here that my objections to Warren's
characters are too procrustean. For certainly it is possible
to take the position that all literature of all periods is to a
greater or less degree existential, and as for the age under
discussion, there is the example of Henry Fleming, who, if

we can get around all the talk of Christian symbolism in
*The Red Badge of Courage*, is in some ways as fine a figure
of existential hero as we could demand. Men have always
had to make commitments, endure crises, achieve accom-
modations with impending death. But self-consciousness
and the quality thereof count for a great deal. If the existential posture is to have any limits, then we must recognize the difference between those who postulate the absur-
dity of the world, the lack of identity, the loss of freedom,
and others who take other views of the common human
agony. Which is to say, existentialism is a way of looking
at men and life, not a mere foreknowledge of mortality.

But it is a grim way of looking and it exacts its price. As
Helmut Kuhn put it, in what seems to me a brilliant figure,
the existentialist takes the road to Calvary, but when he
gets there he finds only the crosses of the two thieves. A
true belief in such a nothingness lacks both the dignity and
the high sense of despair that accrued to our former stances
of negation. It leads to a mock show—Faustus with no
Satan to deal with, no God to betray. Small wonder it is
then that only the very strong—Camus, for example, and
the early Hemingway—can regard emptiness without
flinching and write about it with such stringent fidelity
that every small victory is effected totally from within.
Others require a more promising context, a glimmer of
hope that life may be made easier by means of social action
or political reform. But this, I dare to say in spite of Sar-
tre's vast reputation as writer and thinker, is a marriage
of ideas that contradict and strive against each other. If
the world is truly meaningless, then its nothingness is absolute and unalterable: if, on the other hand, the human
condition and the frame which defines it are subject to

melioration, then the universal emptiness is not complete. Consequently, images that argue against each other tend to cancel each other, and in *Band of Angels*, this damaging contention manifests itself in a weakening of motivation which grows more serious as the narrative proceeds.

After the second major climax, when Amantha turns in disgust from Hamish Bond who has just told her the story of his past, the emphasis shifts from the private suffering of Amantha to the public ordeal of the Civil War. This is a common practice of the historical novelist. If his public and private actions are properly amalgamated, if his character is truly drawn in terms of the historical context, then it is essential to the scope and success of the work that the smaller, private images participate in and at best become one with the larger configurations which have been constructed out of the alarms and exigencies of the past. But once Amantha has left Bond, escaped from slavery, and married Sears, the credible reasons for her anxiety are removed. She has as much identity and as much freedom as are commonly thought to be necessary. Yet out of some brooding sense of her unhappy past, some lingering agony, she abandons Sears to follow Rau-Ru, now become Lieutenant Oliver Cromwell Jones. We are to interpret this as an effort which Amantha makes to discover her ultimate self in terms of her vestigial black blood. The Freudian overtones, her fascination with Jones's shape and color, her obsessive desire to see the scars on his back do not make her flight to him more believable. She simply goes while the reader wonders why, and all the while the story is held together, allowed to happen by the historical situation which produces the chaos that will partially mask the lack of motive and the violence which keeps the novel moving

along. Once Amantha has married Sears, his conduct alone
makes sense. At this juncture, he comes close to knowing
who he is, and his desire is to do good, to improve the conditions of human existence through political commitment
and sacrificial devotion to programs of social change. His
actions fit the dimensions of history in the last part of the
novel even better, perhaps, than Amantha's predicament
was symbolized by the larger milieu of the first. But Amantha remains the principal character of the novel, and she no
longer functions in terms of the book's main historical
thrust.

All this brings me to a fatally simple question: can existentialism as we commonly define and practice it ever furnish the historical novelist with a proper thematic basis
for his work? I am aware as I ask this that our concept
of the existential may be deeply flawed. For example,
Jacques Maritain warns us that anguish has no philosophical standing. It is not a function of Cartesian analysis, nor is it the stuff of a premise to be cast into an
Hegelian figure. Rather, it is an emotion which is essentially religious: it represents a subjective cry unto the
transcendent. When it is properly understood, according
to Maritain, the existentialism of Kierkegaard, Kafka,
Chestov, and others issues from the "nothingness which
is the nonbeing *in* the existent," which is to say in the individual, rather than from any universal meaninglessness
which imposes the terms of the human condition from
without. I find Maritain's interpretation appealing, but I
am conscious that his is a minority report. In any event,
whatever the proper meaning of existentialism may be,
Warren and virtually all his contemporaries are certain
that the nothingness resides *outside* the existent and that

there is no God to call out to, and that the transcendent, in whatever form or dimension, does not exist.

And because life is change and nothing remains stable, our posited nothingness, be it real or imagined, closes in. Our possibilities, the choices that are available to us both in life and in fiction, are diminished; because regardless of the claims that have been made to the contrary, the death of God has grievously reduced mankind. If there is nothing beyond ourselves, and if, as we are told time and time again these days, our first duty is the simple physical perpetuation of our species, then soon there will not be anything to write about or even to concern ourselves with except whether we live or die. But I shall not dwell on this. I merely want to say that existential philosophy imposes restrictions of theme and vision on the novelist. And while it may be true that those who write about their own time cannot avoid either the philosophy or the accompanying restrictions, the historical novelist can and should.

I alluded earlier to the aesthetic or psychic distance the historical image affords the novelist, but there is a moral or philosophical distance to be achieved as well. The novelist who writes of the past is freed of the prejudices and disagreements and idiocies of the moment: he goes back into time and thereby relieves himself and his readers of their predispositions. Only the characters have a stake in the action or the outcome. The artistic vision is purified, so that, ideally at least, man and his condition are more clearly seen. Warren has given us an example of this, not only in the Cass Mastern section of *All the King's Men*, but in his first novel, *Night Rider*, which many critics consider one of his finest works. It will be recalled that *Night Rider* is based on the often violent struggle between the

tobacco growers' association and the organized tobacco
buyers which took place in Tennessee and Kentucky just
prior to and around the time Warren was born. By 1939,
when the novel was published, this was a part of the dead
past: a solution had been found to the tobacco problem
and the old wounds had healed.

Curiously, Warren says in a note at the front of *Night
Rider* that although the story is based on actual events, the
book is not an historical novel, but I think it is easy to
guess what he means. I take it that he is disclaiming any
interest in the surface attractions of history and empha-
sizing his concern with human nature itself which is the
novelist's proper province. The main character in *Night
Rider*, Percy Munn, is a lawyer who allows himself, almost against his will, to become involved in the tobacco
growers' protest. In the course of the novel we watch
Munn's deterioration. As Munn becomes more deeply involved with the association, he increasingly subordinates
his individual responsibility to the will of the group. He
gives up both his right and his duty to make his own moral
choices, which is to say that he abdicates his birthright as
a man. For Munn, one act of evil leads to another; as his
sins increase in severity and number, all aspects of his life
disintegrate into disorder; thus the book moves with inexorable power toward Munn's death at the end. *Night
Rider* is more than a sum of its parts: it transcends its
images in a way that *Band of Angels* never does. And yet,
like *Band of Angels*, it takes the question of human freedom for its theme. The difference is that Munn begins free,
and as a result of his own weakness and poor judgment,
he loses his freedom and therefore loses humanity, and
we in turn believe in and are moved by his death. Amantha begins postulating a lack of freedom, but except for

her interlude of enslavement, this is only something we are told about, and it is hard to see how she is much freer on the last page than she was on the first.

I suppose what I am saying here is that truth for the historical novelist does not reside in the present, except as the present is a part of the eternal. The truth of history is in the past and always, but not in the restricted contemporary view. Therefore, the historical novelist must trust the historical images and the historical context. He must be willing to work with life as it was lived, knowing that history is indeed life and that human nature does not change. Above all, he must avoid the temptation to impose the errors of the present upon the past. For the present is fraught with errors: the one thing above all else that our secular, scientific culture should have taught us is that we are always wrong. Today's certainty is the instigation of tomorrow's superior smile.

Which brings me again to a point I have been insisting upon: the historical novel, like all other novels, must start with the concrete: it must be built from the bottom, not from the top. For whatever literature has to tell us about our continuing agony and glory, it must show us as individuals first, single people in the here and now, or the there and then of another era. Historical or otherwise, the novelist must start with the scene, because the art of literature is not one of definition or one of gathering proof for principles that are already established in the mind of the author. It is rather a search, an exploration begun and conducted in faith, a voyage toward a shore that is at best dimly seen. Whether we look toward the past or to the present, we must take our chances: we must submit to the risks of the craft, or we fail.

# Katherine Anne Porter:
# The Glories and the Errors
# of Her Ways

If, as we are often told, a writer is as good as his best work, then Katherine Anne Porter is a master of the art of short fiction. Critics may dispute over what she does most skillfully—the story, the novella—or argue which among her finest pieces is the very finest of all, but it is generally agreed that her long and careful career has produced a handful of artistic triumphs. Some of the best criticism of her work was recently collected by Lodwick Hartley and George Core who are themselves astute commentators on the fruits of Miss Porter's genius; and one need not go beyond their table of contents to be reminded of the lavish praise that Miss Porter's writing has received from some of our most perceptive and demanding practitioners. Think, for example, of Robert Penn Warren's "Irony With a Center," which Hartley and Core refer to as a "classic of criticism." More than that, it is a classic of the New Criticism, and for me, at least, it demonstrates anew how very much that now belabored method can disclose to us about a work of literature.

I have no wish to go over ground that must be familiar
to anyone who has read anything at all about Miss Porter's
achievement, but Warren's piece, which is now almost
thirty years old, retains an astonishing freshness. This is
not only a tribute to his skill as critic, but testimony, too,
of the sound structure and clean technical accomplishment
of such stories as "Flowering Judas" and "Noon Wine."
For it is true, as Warren tells us, that Braggioni's corpu-
lence, his clothes, his scarred flesh convey a sense of the
man that leads us toward the meaning of the whole story,
and perhaps to the heart of the common motive behind all
Miss Porter's work: that "tissue of contradictions" which
is mankind. Warren is superb at disclosing the meaning
of every slight detail, the nuances of what appears to be
casual conversation—for nothing can be really casual in
a properly executed story—and the emotions that produce
a gesture of the hand or a flick of the eye. He has few
peers at this sort of practice, but one of them is certainly
Cleanth Brooks, who is represented in the Hartley-Core
volume by a short essay on "The Grave."

Brooks thinks that this story, perhaps better than any
other, "illustrates [Miss Porter's] genius as a writer," and
though other critics lean toward longer works such as
"Pale Horse, Pale Rider" or "Old Mortality," Brooks's
selection of "The Grave" is difficult to fault. For one thing,
the story successfully carries a great weight of symbolism
for so short a work. In the course of less than a dozen
pages, Miss Porter encompasses the inexorable progress
of all life—from birth to love and on to death, from ignorance to self-discovery, from alienation to sympathy with
the rest of the doomed and suffering world. She uses some
graves, a wedding ring, a silver dove, a dead, pregnant

rabbit, and at the end, sweets made in the shapes of animals, to convey her theme in its complexity, and the story
sustains all this because characteristically, Miss Porter
has paid careful attention to the smallest details of her
craft. Who else could get away with such an ending? With
the indentation that starts a new paragraph, she transcends, at the very close of the narrative, more than twenty
years. As Brooks is able to demonstrate, such a sudden
shift in time is made possible by the consummate success
of all that has gone before. And the symbols are enhanced
in "richness and subtlety" by the later, foreign context in
which they are finally seen.

Nor do all of Miss Porter's admirers employ the meth-
ods of the New Criticism. Eudora Welty for example is
concerned with the metaphysics of the stories, and she
cannot discover in Miss Porter's fiction the sharp clarity
of image and detail that Warren and Brooks celebrate as
the keystone of her success. According to Miss Welty, we
do not "see" Miss Porter's stories happen, and Miss Welty
doubts whether Miss Porter sees them, either. The narratives are told to us, and they transpire not in Texas or
Germany or Mexico, but "on a stage of her own." "She is
writing stories of the spirit," Miss Welty says, "and the
time that fills those moments is eternity." This is high
praise, but by the time Miss Welty got around to making
it, the reaction was beginning to set in.

It is curious, looking back, to see what a charmed life
Miss Porter lived. Clearly, the rumor of the big novel that
was to come—so long in the process of creation, so often
delayed—kept the question of the scantiness of her canon
from arising. It hardly seemed proper to say that Miss
Porter had not written very much, since so much more—

the crowning achievement of her genius—was not yet published. Even those who found a kind of thinness in the stories, who saw them drained, if not of life, at least of greatness by Miss Porter's will to achieve surface perfection, were obliged to reserve judgment, lest the novel prove them wrong. But at last the novel appeared, to the fanfare of publicity trumpets and torrents of overpraise, and it turned out to be an embarrassment to many of Miss Porter's most enthusiastic partisans. As I shall attempt to show later, *Ship of Fools* is a bad book. And the danger now, as I see it, is that we might overreact. Looking at this seriously flawed and strangely dead novel, we might be tempted to minimize Miss Porter's accomplishment by allowing her earlier work to fall under the shadow of her more recent failure.

And indeed, fate, which was for so long kind to Miss Porter, and bad judgment, which neither she nor her publishers have demonstrated before, have now conspired to make our harsh pronouncements easier for us. What I have in mind is the publication by Seymour Lawrence of Miss Porter's *Collected Essays and Other Occasional Writings*, which I am sorry to say lays the worst parts of Miss Porter's mind and soul bare before the world. That the book should have been published is, I suppose, understandable. At best, we can blame ourselves, our professional curiosities that demand to know everything, that insist on having every scrap, every jot and tittle that ever came from the artist's pen to help form the base of our scholarship and criticism. Mr. Lawrence knows the ways of the literary world, of course, and he was doubtless thinking of his balance sheet. But what, we may ask, was Miss Porter thinking of?

I do not know, and it will be cruel for me to speculate—
though I shall have to bring myself to do so before I
am done. But I recall, in this connection, a story Randall
Stewart used to tell, of a young man at an MLA meeting
who declared his wish that all biographical and personal
data about all writers, past, present, and future, might be
irretrievably mislaid. This was an excessive desire, to be
sure, engendered, some will say, by an overdose of the New
Criticism. But I remember another meeting where Floyd
Stovall described the drabness inherent in editing Whit-
man's correspondence when toward the end, the utter-
ances of this great man had almost exclusively to do with
the state of his bowels. I do not presume to adjudicate,
but I do raise the question: Must *everything* be published?
Would literature not have been served as well if Miss
Porter's manuscripts and letters and fragments and effu-
sions had been kept for the use of scholars at the University of Maryland library and not thrust upon the public
view? I raise the question. And yet, I am aware that reading Miss Porter's occasional pieces has helped to confirm
and perhaps even enlighten my original judgment of *Ship
of Fools*. And I am afraid they can be made to bear even
more damaging witness in the appraisals of unfriendly
commentators such as John W. Aldridge.

Aldridge is a sound and reasonable critic, and he demonstrates to my satisfaction that Miss Porter is essentially
a southern writer who is at her best when she is writing
about the homeland and people that she best knows. "Old
Mortality," Aldridge thinks, is better than "Flowering
Judas," and in his final judgment, he feels that Miss Porter
has cheated herself and created less well and less substan-
tially than she might have done by pursuing an ideal of

artistic perfection rather than allowing her passions free
rein in the tradition of Faulkner and Wolfe. This opinion
is borne out by the occasional writings. By far the best
thing in *The Collected Essays* is "Portrait: Old South," a
memoir of Miss Porter's grandmother, which brings to
sympathetic life not only the old lady and the family over
which she was matriarch, but the entire world in which
she lived in all its spiritual and societal and historical dimensions. Less good, but still lively and even touching are
a piece about St. Francisville, Louisiana, and an account
of her first meeting with Eudora Welty. But Miss Welty
is a writer, and there is nothing like another author—or
even the rumor of one—to bring out Miss Porter's self-
centeredness. She condescends—there is no other word for
it—to Miss Welty, to Flannery O'Connor, to Hemingway
and Ford Madox Ford, and finally, though in a subtle way,
to T. S. Eliot.

Judged on the basis of the evidence she gives us in *Collected Essays*, Miss Porter is very egotistical, which does
not distinguish her to any great extent from other writers
or from the human race in general. Who was vainer than
Joyce? Or than Faulkner, one imagines, if the truth were
told? But there are these differences and I see them as in-
structive. Joyce, aside from his talent as a writer, was an
intellectual giant who had been handsomely educated. His
mind, directed toward himself as it always was, nonetheless moved in channels unavailable to lesser mortals, and
for fellow travelers the journey is joyful and enlightening.
One reads Joyce's letters and learns how grand and curious and unpredictable and even funny were the workings
of his cerebral processes. His ego assumes its place in the
context of his character, and the force of his learning and

his perception carries him and us along. As for Faulkner, for most of his life he was too busy writing novels to make a fool of himself.

But to put the matter bluntly, Miss Porter is quickly out of her intellectual depth, and she flounders in currents that swirl above her head without seeming to realize that she has lost her footing. Her judgments, literary and otherwise, are made from the heart, from the same passionate center, as Aldridge suggests, which generated her magnificent Texas stories. But Miss Porter's heart is essentially romantic, and it cannot know why Thomas Hardy is a good novelist, and it feels imperiled by the learning of a man such as Eliot, and above all, it wants to tell of itself, to sing its own praises and to damn those who might want to share the stage. Thus it fails to make proper distinctions: to distinguish, for example, between the propriety of publishing a perfectly legitimate, though not brilliant, piece of criticism on Gertrude Stein and an exchange of letters about Miss Stein that are motivated by hurt pride and which are intensely personal and bitterly derogatory.

Again and again, reading *The Collected Essays*, one is struck by the narrowness of Miss Porter's view and her willingness to accept as final wisdom whatever cliché comes to hand. At one extreme is her *Ladies' Home Journal* piece, bad even for that magazine, on Jacqueline Kennedy. However much we may have been grieved by the death of the President or blinded by our own ideological fervor, the writer's job is to tell the truth, and the first truth of all is that nobody is perfect. But Miss Porter, like the sob sisters in the popular press, thought Mrs. Kennedy was, and she sets out to tell us so in terms that are unbelievably fulsome.

Jackie, we are told, is "lionhearted," she has a "sweet and merry," but not a "weak face," she "lived hourly in love and joy, yet with every duty done and every demand fulfilled: nothing overlooked or neglected." I hope I will not be accused of political bias or sour disappointment at Mrs. Kennedy's more recent domestic liaison, when I say, in answer to this last assertion, that I seriously doubt it. But beyond Miss Porter's dream of Mrs. Kennedy's flawless character lies an inability to separate the moral wheat from the social chaff. No distinction is made between Mrs. Kennedy's superb composure in the face of tragic bereavement and her skill in selecting a dress or applying her makeup: all is one mirror of perfection, and so all is false.

On the other hand, chapters from Miss Porter's unfinished work on the Mather family are included in the *Essays*, and here the main figures are villains and therefore black to the core. Nowhere, except perhaps in *Ship of Fools*, do Miss Porter's simplicity of ideational conception and catch-as-catch-can education damage her performance more than when she is dealing with these eccentric, frequently unfathomable, but undeniably brilliant divines. She has no desire to try to understand them psychologically and no power by which she can attempt to understand them intellectually, so she makes straw men of them. She becomes a hunter of witch hunters, which is—or at least was—the order of the day. Her method is familiar: clinging to her own place in history, evoking every prejudice of her own milieu, she denies the Mathers theirs. They must be seen by totally modern eyes, and judged absolutely by Miss Porter's terms and not by their own.

I pass now from this painful collection—the letters to the *Washington Post* and the *Village Voice*, the memoirs

of houses Miss Porter has lived in and the bad poems about
death and love—and turn to the novel and what some critics have said about it. Robert Heilman has written of style,
of Miss Porter's ability to use language, to make the words
work to convey shades of character and implications of
event. This is one of the greater parts of her talent and
it never abandons her. So far, so good. More ambitiously,
M. M. Liberman, noting the poor reception that the book
got from serious critics, has attempted a full-scale defense
of *Ship of Fools*, and he bases his case on what he considers a commonplace of literary criticism: "If a literary
work is more than immediately engaging, if, for example,
it stimulates the moral imagination, it is doing more than
is fairly required of it as art." That Mr. Liberman's commonplace may not after all be so commonly held is evident
to a good many critics I can think of, and to Mr. Liberman,
apparently, for he makes a spirited attack on those who
dissent from his proposition.

And I am one of them. Without arguing the question,
as Mr. Liberman himself does not argue it, I offer a couple
of counterpropositions which seem to me to be commonplace. First, literature is a moral art in that it deals with
questions of moral significance. It would seem to follow
that given two equally competent formal presentations,
the work with the more profound and universal moral in-
volvements would be superior. But putting the moral quali-
fications aside, from a purely intellectual point of view,
the idea does matter. The work of the mind, the purely
cerebral notions that are conveyed are certainly not everything, but they just as certainly help to make "Goe and
catch a falling star" a better poem than "Star light, star
bright." And so I think one thing that happened to Miss

Porter in *Ship of Fools* and in "The Leaning Tower," and to a smaller degree in some of her other fiction, is that neither her conscious nor her subconscious mind was capable of dealing with the complexities of the themes she had chosen.

This is a view that I think I share with Lodwick Hartley. His "Dark Voyagers," points out Miss Porter's inability to deal with her own material or to bring the various groupings and impulses of character and plot to any kind of coherence of meaningful discovery. Miss Porter's best character has always been herself, and as Hartley points out, in spite of her claim to the contrary—"I am the captain and the seasick bulldog. . . ."—she cannot *be* all the people in *Ship of Fools* at once, and therefore most of the characterizations fail. But these flaws are well known and I shall not dwell on them. Rather, let me revert to a point I made earlier. She seized the cliché of evil Germany, and then she extended the evil to include all mankind: the Americans, the Swiss, the Latins: by an easy extrapolation, all who make a progress through this vale of tears. And of course we are all evil—I do not forget my objection to Jackie Kennedy's perfection—but we are not all equally evil, nor are we evil in the same ways, nor do our evils cause the same amount of anguish. I think a consciousness of these differences is of overwhelming importance to a literary performance, creative or critical: an understanding of our moral and spiritual inequality is basic to our comprehension of the general human condition.

So it will not do to imply that America is and was as guilty as Germany. There is no sane way to compare, say, the relocation of Japanese-Americans after Pearl Harbor

with Hitler's efforts to exterminate the Jews. One may
agree that life is all of a piece, a single tapestry, but the
picture it presents is varicolored: some of the threads are
dun and some are gold. And so it was, so it had to be,
even in Germany when the Nazi horror raged at its worst.
And, after all, novels are not written about nations any
more than they are written about abstractions. One does
not write a book about love, but about people who are in
love. Tolstoy did not write a book about Russia, but about
the Bezukhovs and the Bolkonskis and all the rest, and it
is because he wrote so well about them that the book
achieves its national character. The delineations of the
individual humans, some of whom are reasonably good
even under the worst government, and in the worst society, must come first.

Thomas Mann, whose animosity toward the German
people was often extravagant, knew this. Speculation is
idle, and more than that, unfair, but I wonder if *Doctor
Faustus* is not really the kind of book that Miss Porter
was after when she composed *Ship of Fools*. I find Mann's
novel difficult and in many ways distasteful, but who could
deny that it is a literary work of the highest merit? Everything is there: the pervading sense of absolute evil, the
universal depravity of man. But the human differences are
emphasized and the metaphysical dimension gives the book
both depth and scope. Mann was a gentleman of truly vast
learning, and so such a book as *Doctor Faustus* was clearly
out of Miss Porter's—and almost everybody else's—reach.
But I wonder that she did not feel the need, if not for
God or Satan, at least for the kind of human will and
desire and affection that carry human existence beyond
the strictly mundane.

For if Mann is too stern a comparison to ask Miss Porter to face, then turn to Thomas Wolfe who understood, in connection with the German question, the necessity for love. It seems to me that one of the finest things Wolfe ever wrote was "I Have a Thing to Tell You," in *You Can't Go Home Again*. Admittedly, this work was done long before the full magnitude of Hitler's racial policy was known either inside or outside Germany and indeed before it was put into effect in all its hideous dimensions. This may have made it easier for Wolfe to achieve the complexity of characterization and outlook that he demonstrates in this sequence. But Miss Porter had the same advantage when she wrote "The Leaning Tower," and this story fails in much the same way as *Ship of Fools*. The ambivalence of feeling in "I Have a Thing to Tell You," the essentially decent people who find themselves too morally depleted to fight the dark wave that is engulfing them; the sense of helplessness and confusion and deep sorrow along with all the evil; the foreboding that announces the end of something, the passing of a kind of beauty that the world will never know again—all of this is in Wolfe. Our hearts are wrenched, and we are impelled on toward the greater monstrosity which is too vast to be directly approached or ultimately encompassed.

Mann, with all of his incredible knowledge, built from the top, and with the sheer power of his mind which taxes the reader on every page, he brought *Doctor Faustus* to its cold fruition. Wolfe, working as was his habit, not so much by design as from his insight into the human temperament, achieved what I think all writers must achieve if they are finally to be successful. He saw people sternly and with great sympathy; he despised the sin, but he loved the

sinner. This, one thinks, Miss Porter might have done if
she had gone about her task in a different way and had a
clearer vision of the nature of her own talents. But she
did not, and at this point in time, her big novel seems to
have hurt her reputation more than it has helped it.

And we may go one step further. The struggle between
Miss Porter's head and her heart has, I believe, damaged
to a small degree some of those stories that are generally
held to be successful. Warren makes a persuasive case for
the end of "Old Mortality," but the weight of critical opinion is on the other side. The work closes on a note not so
much of uncertainty as of falseness. Through all its previous sequences "Old Mortality" is filled with the richness
of life—with love and disappointment, with pain and fulfillment and mystery; and it is against this mystery, the
high romance that informs and surrounds the myth of
Amy, that the attempts to explain the story and life itself
in terms of mere psychology clatter and fail. In my judgment, something like this happens in some of the shorter
pieces—"The Circus," for example, and "The Jilting of
Granny Weatherall," where the tight structure and the
almost total realization of the warmth and complexity of
life are infringed, if only slightly, by an effort to explain.

Yet, it is probably unfair to say, as Aldridge does suggest, that Miss Porter should have trusted her emotions
more and followed her memory in its purity, or to express
the wish, as I have above, that she might have better understood her weaknesses and strengths. In the final analysis, writers—if they are serious, as Miss Porter is serious,
and willing to suffer the requisite agony, as she unquestionably has been willing to suffer—writers who are faithful do the best they can. She has followed her heart as far

as it would take her, and in one sense, it was while she was trying to follow it even further that it played her false. It could not be and therefore she could not be a microcosm of the world. But it gave us "Noon Wine" and "Pale Horse, Pale Rider" and several other small masterpieces. It is because these are so very fine that we dare complain that she did not give us more.

# Southern Novelists and the Civil War

I suppose there must be someone in the world, some careful scholar good at such things, who knows, at least in rough figures, how many novels have been written about the American Civil War. Fifteen years ago, Robert Lively was able to list over five hundred which had been produced by Southerners alone. How many have been written by Northerners, I cannot say, but it seems safe to affirm that in spite of *The Red Badge of Courage* and a few other startling successes in the field, the war remains largely a southern province. Most of the big names of the renascence made use of it: Faulkner, of course, and Warren to a certain extent; Caroline Gordon, Andrew Lytle, Allen Tate, Stark Young. More recently, the production of Civil War literature has tapered off. Flannery O'Connor did not write about it. Neither has Styron or Madison Jones or George Garrett or Walker Percy, and it is easy to guess why: the voice of the romantic past has been all but silenced, if only temporarily, by the agonies of race.

Whatever other reasons lay behind the war, it was

fought to perpetuate slavery, and this is the historical fact that can be most easily grasped. Those among us who have time and inclination for such things may speculate over the paradoxes and ambiguities of the southern character, how Lee and a lot of other Confederates hated slavery but felt obligated to fight for their section; but given the world we now live in with its ideological polarizations, its thrust toward intellectual conformity and the recurrent crises of racial strife, we must choose sides against Lee or suffer the consequences. I suspect that Percy and Styron and Jones and Garrett—not O'Connor, who was her own woman first and last—would be better novelists if they had been born and begun to write sooner, and I suspect all of them would have searched for their imagery in the Civil War. For all of us, and so particularly for the artist, many of the keys to our understanding of the present lie in the past. What locks the keys fit and what shadows lie behind the doors that are opened—all this is the complex stuff of art and therefore subject to enormous disagreement. That is, we may interpret the past in a thousand different ways, but we must know that it exists, that it has an objective and complicated reality, and we must comprehend as many of its facets as our vision can encompass.

I am inclined to think that as far as literature is concerned—southern literature, anyway—the war will always be with us. It is not quite obliterated now: it exists around the periphery of every southern novel; it makes its appearance in quaint old ladies and portraits above the fireplace and monuments on the squares. It is a part of us, and someday we shall have to turn back to it, if only in an effort to understand more fully the painful time we are now living through which will then be the past. I have a

dream of our literary future. I envision a new golden age
of uncertainty, a time when the writer no longer knows
any final answers to mundane problems or solutions to our
cultural dislodgements and social concerns. Then he may
assume his proper business of discovery, which means
that he will have to consider Lee once more and perhaps
reread *The Fathers* by Allen Tate.

It is perhaps easiest to begin with Mr. Tate's book because of all modern Civil War novelists he is the only one
who completely defined his position on the South and the
Civil War some years before he wrote his novel. I do not
mean to imply that *The Fathers* is in any way redundant.
The values of Tate's novel are not precisely those found
in "Ode to the Confederate Dead," and the book has its
meanings beyond those which are stated in the essays on
southern literature and culture. But in 1938, when the
book was published—or for that matter in any subsequent
year—many readers must have approached *The Fathers*
with definite notions concerning Mr. Tate's view of the
South. One should have known, for example, that Mr. Tate
deplored slavery on the ground that the Negroes did not
function as a proper peasant class, which in turn is the
*sine qua non* of a great culture. Tate considered the southern God to be a spurious God, an alien borrowed from
sixteenth-century merchants; and he deemed the plutoc-
racy of the North and the aristocracy of the South to be
similar in their essential qualities. Most important of all
was Tate's distinction between the Long View and the
Short View of history. For the Long View is "the religion
of the half horse," and only the Short View—that way of
seeing history as an image or a number of images—can

provide the artist with a foundation on which to build his world.

To the southern writer who would deal with the past, the Civil War is the most significant image of all. For it is the pregnant moment in southern history, that instant which contains within its own limits a summation of all that has gone before, an adumbration of the future. To put it another way, the war is important not merely in itself, but in what it implies; for at the hands of a skillful artist, the single image may be made to convey an entire civilization and the moral code on which that civilization was constructed. Indeed, in many Civil War novels the actual conflict exists only as a background against which certain ramifications of the traditional southern code are developed.

Lionel Trilling in a review of *The Fathers* affords an excellent example of the sort of misunderstanding that results from the use of the Long View of history as a critical principle. Mr. Trilling took Major Buchan to be a representative of the old order, and he saw Major Buchan's limited Virginia world as a microcosm of the traditional society of the South. George Posey he understood as a symbol of northern industrialism, and the conflict of the novel was joined with the meeting of these two forces. This is, as far as it goes, a legitimate reading of *The Fathers*, but Mr. Trilling had one complaint to make. He could not see that Mr. Tate had *logically proved* the superiority of the traditional society over the culture that Posey represented. There was, he said, only Mr. Tate's fine and sensitive writing about the Buchans, which was, ultimately, no kind of proof at all. In other words, the novel contained no abstract theory, but merely a grand image. Mr. Tate had taken the Short View.

The central image of *The Fathers* is the Buchan family group including on one hand a dead grandfather and on the other the in-law, George Posey, and from beginning to end, the essential qualities of the image do not vary. I do not mean by this simply that the closing events of the book are prepared for in the opening pages. Certainly, this is true. But of more importance is the fact that the destructive element, that weakness of the southern culture which leads toward doom, is visibly present within the ordered precincts of the family. The reader's progress through the novel, the way of the book itself, is that of discovery; we are allowed to see, one after another, the various faces of the image, and we come to understand the truth of it in the end.

Posey is not only a part of the central image but also a manifestation of a rudimentary weakness in the culture of the South. If he seems out of place in the southern tradition, he does so simply because we have come erroneously to believe that Henry Grady was the first traitor to the agrarian ideal. For the reasons that Mr. Tate has given us, we should know better. Grandfather Buchan, the dead ancestor who comes to life in the final pages, points out that Posey could not have existed in his, the grandfather's, eighteenth-century world. "The only expectancy that he shares with humanity is the pursuing grave," the old man says, "and the thought of extinction overwhelms him because he is entirely alone. My son, in my day we were never alone." But Grandfather Buchan goes further. He tells the story of Jason and the Golden Fleece, more clearly to define the nature of Posey's defection, and to show that

evil breeds without fail in any vacuum that is created by
the absence of good. Posey's intention is morally neutral.
The intention of the antebellum society was good. But
there were rents in its armor, gaps in the philosophy on
which it was built. This is evident at the beginning of the
novel.

When we see Major Buchan and Posey together for the
first time, they are locked in battle, and the issue is re-
solved in Posey's favor. Posey wins because he will not
abide by the rules, he will not conduct himself in accordance with inherited standards. This reading of southern
literature as the story of traditional men who must either
violate their own code or suffer defeat is one that has been
suggested many times before. But not enough attention
has been given to the underlying reason for the failure of
the traditional southern culture. We cannot believe, of
course, that in this world victory is always with the right,
but neither are we justified in assuming that the warrior
unrestrained by rules will always overcome the man who
fights by an ethical code. Grandfather Buchan's society
was as ordered as that of the major; its code was as strict.
But the culture of late eighteenth-century Virginia was
powerful enough to hold in abeyance the spirit that motivated Posey. This was so because the southern weakness
of believing that the highest good of man is the good of
politics had not, before 1861, developed to its destructive
logical conclusion.

Major Buchan was a religious man, and on the eve of
the Civil War he read in his morning prayer the alter-
native version of the Episcopal service which was pro-
vided in the book for use when calamity threatened the
family. But this final decision to cast his lot with the Union

was a moral judgment made according to political theory rather than Christian theology. That is to say, he looked to Thomas Jefferson to find out what was right and then prayed to God to strengthen his resolution. He was doomed in the end to be defeated by Posey and all that Posey represented not because he lived by traditional rules, but because the tradition itself was founded on a political and not a religious ethic.

As the narrator, Lacy Buchan, puts it, "I cannot to this day decide just how papa looked at it: whether in his mind the domestic trials, growing out of my mother's death, were one thing, and the public crisis another. Nor can I decide in my own mind whether it was possible to distinguish the two—they worked together for a single evil, and I think the evil was the more overwhelming among us because of the way men had of seeing themselves at that time: as in all highly developed societies the line marking off the domestic from the public life was indistinct." The war must be understood as the climax of southern culture, the last moment of order in a traditional society. Before 1861 the inherited code of the South remained an adequate guide for ethical conduct—the existence of all the George Poseys notwithstanding. After 1865 the old morality was no longer sufficient to serve as a valid standard of behavior. Therefore, the war, taken alone without reference to the tradition, is meaningless. It functions in the southern novel as a dramatic symbol; in a sense, it is the catastrophe at the end of the play, the agony that rises out of moral imperfections.

Andrew Lytle's *The Long Night*, which appeared in 1936, is a first novel, written with amazing skill and constructed with a great deal of subtlety. The main charac-

ter of *The Long Night* is a young man named Pleasant
McIvor, and the story divides itself into two, almost equal
parts. The initial half of Mr. Lytle's book is concerned
with McIvor's quest for revenge. Aided occasionally by
relatives, but operating mostly alone, Pleasant sets out to
kill every member of a large band of speculators who have
murdered his father. There follows a series of climaxes as
Mr. Lytle brings to full development, one after another, a
list of characters and allows each in turn to fall victim to
McIvor's steadfast purpose. But at the final moment, when
Pleasant has his gun levelled at the leader of the thieves,
the direction of the novel suddenly changes. The Civil
War has been declared, and on hearing this, McIvor leaves
the chief villain alive, swears to kill him at some future
time, and goes off to join the Confederate Army. From
here on, the emphasis of the story is shifted. There are
further murders by Pleasant, it is true, but very quickly
the cause of revenge is superseded by the greater purpose
of the war until the two themes are brought together
again in the final pages of the novel.

I have outlined the story in order to show that the uni-
fying element of the novel is its thematic structure. For
if one examines the book with a view that does not see
beyond the plot, he will discover certain frailties, certain
breaks in continuity, and shifts in intention that appear
on the surface to be flaws. The single motive of the narrative seems to dissipate in the last half of the novel, a
new set of characters is introduced, a whole new world is
drawn. Obviously the book shifts direction when the war
begins: the continuity of plot and setting are broken: the
action moves off along a totally new line. Or so it seems
until the themes of parts one and two join to make a

whole. In the early sections of *The Long Night* there are
two important images: the McIvor family and the band
of speculators headed by Tyson Lovell. The image of the
family is central to the novel, and it is one which Mr. Lytle
has very carefully unified. Certainly, the meeting of the
McIvor clan is one of the finest scenes in the book; it is
the sort of thing that Mr. Lytle does with great skill. But
its primary purpose is to establish the integrity of the
family, to show the group itself as a moral force. There is
an overall harmony of feeling among those at the gathering which transcends individual differences concerning
the proper method for obtaining justice.

When the meeting is ended and Pleasant, with help from
an uncle and a cousin, starts on his work of vengeance, he
is acting in accordance with the general will of the family.
That is to say, he is fulfilling a domestic, a private obligation. Further, the family duty, as the McIvors see it,
coincides precisely with the public responsibility—that of
ridding the community of murderers and thieves. Even
the method, execution, is the same. All of this changes
abruptly, however, when we are introduced to the Civil
War, the third and final image of the book. In the first
chapter, which deals directly with the Confederate Army,
Pleasant kills four of his ancient enemies, but the consequences of his act, under the new war conditions, become
immediately apparent. He must pretend that his comrades
were victims of the enemy and thereby give false intelligence to his commanders. The war develops; we are treated
to a magnificent handling of the Battle of Shiloh; and with
each page the breach between public and private duty
widens. The old ethic, based on political considerations, is
inadequate to cope with this new, unforseen moral situa-

tion. Armistead McIvor, Pleasant's cousin, recognizes this
and advises the boy to forget about his revenge. But Pleasant clings to his purpose.

In one of the last scenes of the book, Pleasant neglects
his responsibility as a scout in order to attempt another of
his acts of retribution. He moves close to one of his enemies, raises his pistol, and finds that he cannot shoot. He
has come to knowledge; he has discovered the significance
of the war and the imperfection of his moral position. But
he sees, too, that his understanding has come too late.
Pleasant's military defection is the direct cause of Ellis
Roswell's death. Adherence to private duty has damaged
both the public and private good. The end is renunciation:
of the living and the dead, of war and vengeance, of the
old, traditional order by which he had lived.

Caroline Gordon's *None Shall Look Back*, which was
published in 1941, is perhaps of all southern novels the
sternest and most unrelenting in its treatment of the Civil
War. For at the conclusion of the book, every single character who has remained constant to the southern ethic has
either been killed or sadly broken. Rives Allard, George
Rowan, and Spencer Rowe are dead; Ned's health is per-
manently impaired by months of prison life; Fountain Allard has lost his reason as the result of a severe stroke.
Except in the cases of Belle Allard and Love Minor, there
is nothing but bereavement and a kind of hopeless bitter-
ness among the women. Of all the immediate Allard connection, only Jim, who represents the spirit of commerce,
is seen to thrive in the end.

It would be superfluous to do more than point out the
fact that here again the principal image is the family and
that the public and private moralities coincide until the

*status quo* is ruptured by the war. Fountain Allard knows
that what is good for the land is good for his own children
and his own slaves and for all the community at large.
This is well conveyed in the chapters that deal with his
morning ride over the plantation at Brackets and his investigation of the overseer's cruelty at Cabin Row. But of
more importance to the success of Miss Gordon's novel is
the development of the character Rives Allard. He refuses
to live beyond the failure of his inherited moral code.

Andrew Lytle, in his essay on Miss Gordon's work,
finds that the main theme of *None Shall Look Back* is the
young man's pursuit of death. There is much in the text
of the novel to substantiate this view, and early in the
story the careful reader must certainly be aware that
Rives will not survive the war. When he is leaving Donel-
son with Forrest's cavalry, riding past the wounded over
the frozen ground, his eye is caught by one of the injured,
and a moment later he predicts his own end. "The dark
glance had been enigmatic but there had been in it a flicker
of hostility which men look on at unbearable suffering. It
was as if the man dying in the circle of the firelight could
not endure the spectacle of the living, who were only riding toward death." This is the first in a series of incidents
which demonstrate that Rives participates in the knowledge of his ultimate doom.

The sense of mortality is more fully developed through
the consciousness of Lucy. It is she who compares the walls
of the bridal chamber to the sloping sides of a casket. She
feels the chill of death on the ground where recently Rives
has lain; and when a strange Confederate captain dies at
the Allard home, Lucy weeps not for him but for her husband. These are a few examples of the novel's constant

concern with death. There are others of increasing inten-
sity, all of which lead to the final scene between man and
wife, the last evening that Lucy and Rives are together.
In bed with him and wakeful during the night, Lucy has
studied his face. "The light coming in at the window illu-
minated his features: the high, aquiline nose, the eyes
set in their deep hollows, the stern mouth. In the moon-
light they were like marble. The kind of face that might
be carved on a tomb. She drew a quick breath, sank down
beside him, after a little reached over and laid her fingers
on his nerveless hand. It comforted her to find it warm."
Death has begun to take him already. It is as if the chemis-
try of Rives's body has already submitted to a fate it does
not wish to avoid.

This brings us, I think, to the proper center of the novel.
Rives knows as well as Lucy does that he is going to die,
and until the very end he is free to save himself. Late in
1864 even the Negroes knew that the war was lost, and a
Confederate soldier who was at home on leave might have
stayed forever with no fear of being molested by his offi-
cers. Rives rejects his chance to live, not because he loves
death but because he is devoted to the civilization which
he is defending. In so far as she was immediately concerned with the war, per se, Miss Gordon was content to
build her image and then to enhance its value by allowing
a strong man to die for it. Indeed, much of the strength
of the image is personified in the man, and among views
of history, Miss Gordon's is perhaps the shortest one of all.

A novel that is quite different in technique from *None
Shall Look Back* is *So Red the Rose* by Stark Young. This
is a loose, sprawling sort of book which deals with grand
houses and large slaveholders in and around Natchez, Mis-

sissippi. On the basis of a first reading, one has a strong
inclination to dismiss Mr. Young's novel as another moon-
light and magnolia romance, a tale built on the crumbs of
history, anecdotes about famous men which have drifted
down from the past. But such a view of *So Red the Rose*
is less than just. For in spite of the efforts of recent southern writers and historians to minimize the role of the
rich planter in the overall pattern of southern culture, the
great plantations did exist. They were a part of the South,
and they will serve as the stuff for an image.

As is the case in Mr. Young's *Heaven Trees*, everybody
in *So Red the Rose* seems to be related to everybody else
by some ramification of blood or marriage. The family is
the image, and whatever is good or evil in the southern
culture must be found in the glories and failures of the
Mississippi clans. There is much talk in the novel about
politics. Jefferson Davis, himself, is one of the minor characters. But the talk is superficial; Davis is poorly drawn.
Mr. Young fails even to examine the political ethic of the
South. For this reason, the image of *So Red the Rose* is
more strictly limited than that of any other noteworthy
Civil War novel. The book succeeds because the reader is
made to understand the full implications of southern ancestor worship. Late in the novel, when the war is over
and Mississippi is in the hands of carpetbaggers, Hugh
McGehee remembers a story he used to tell to Edward, his
son who died at Shiloh. It is an account of the death of the
Earl of Montrose. The Scottish peer had been a Presby-
terian, and he was betrayed and captured while fighting
for Charles II.

He was to be walked by the bailiffs all along Prince
Street to the Mercat Cross, where the gallows was. In-

stead of his rags, friends had sent him a suit of fine
black cloth, a black beaver hat with a silver band, a scar-
let cloak richly laced to the knee; his stockings were car-
nation silk. He had also, with these, fine white gloves on
his hands and ribbons to his shoes. The mobs had been
hired to mock and howl at him, but when they saw him,
he was so beautiful and grave, there was not a sound, except for their low prayers and tears. He was denied the
privilege always granted, even to common criminals, of
speaking to the crowd. But to those near the scaffold he
spoke a moment, and a boy named Gordon took it down.
". . . drawing near to God. If He enable me to embrace it
even in its most ugly shape, let God be glorified in me,
though it were my damnation."

Hugh saw a little boy listening to this. "So when he
walked along the street like that, Father, there wasn't a
sound," Edward used to say. "No, Buddie," said Lucy, "not
a sound, he was so beautiful. Papa's told you that."

"And we fought for him," Edward said.

The McGehees fought for him, and every McGehee that
came after, down to Edward who died and Lucy who lived
through the travesty of Reconstruction, carried forever
in his mind's eye an image of the Earl of Montrose's
beauty. "But what they would do better to speak of," Hugh
McGehee says later, referring to the people of the South,
"would be not what they have but what they have loved."
Their devotion to a concrete image of the past, their fidelity to a traditional ethic.

This is Mr. Young's thesis, and the method of his novel
is to develop first the code of morality that has been inherited, and second, the love of family and respect for
the past which give the code its practical strength. Therefore, much is made in this book of old portraits and heir-
loom jewels and stories that have been handed down from
father to son. The conduct of the living Bedfords and

McGehees is made significant by Mr. Young's careful attention to the past from which they sprang.

Thomas Sutpen, the main character in William Faulkner's *Absalom, Absalom!*, is as far removed from Hugh
McGehee in background and feeling as Jefferson, the county seat of Mr. Faulkner's Yoknapatawpha, is different
from Natchez and the grand establishments that overlooked the river. Whether or not he was of Scotch descent,
Sutpen himself could not say, and the only past that he
loved was the past that he expected to create for all the
other Sutpens who would come after him. He was born in
the hills of western Virginia, and he turned up in Jefferson in the 1830s having already abandoned his wife and
child and a prosperous establishment in Haiti. He had left
his family because the woman he had married was part
Negro, and he was determined to make of himself a southern gentleman, and to create a line, a dynasty of Sutpens
who would rule in Mississippi as the Tidewater aristocrats
held sway in his native Virginia. He was, in the end, defeated by the son he had rejected, by his own innocence,
by the scope of his own ambitions.

In the final analysis, the war had very little to do with
the frustration of Sutpen's design; indeed, the conflict
was probably responsible for prolonging his hopes four or
five years until the business with the Yankees could be
attended to. But Sutpen has a place in this discussion for
at least two reasons: he may be compared with the Mc-
Gehees and the Buchans, the Allards and the McIvors, to
demonstrate the barren quality of the southern code when
it is assumed and not inherited, when it is regarded outside its context, without benefit of the Short View of history. And in the second place, Sutpen's situation in 1861

was in some respects similar to that of the South as a whole; the rules by which he had guided his life had at last proved less than adequate.

"Sutpen's trouble," Quentin Compson remarked, "was innocence." One of the forms which Sutpen's innocence took was a misunderstanding of spiritual values as material ends. He wanted a family, or, specifically, a son, to carry on the Sutpen name, and it is true that he conceived of his grand design in terms of Sutpens of the past and of the future. But what he knew of the family was simply that every aristocrat had one—ancestors fondly remembered and children nurtured with pride. Of love and duty and fidelity among those who share the same blood, he understood little. So Bon, the son of his first marriage, waited four years in vain, for some sign, some word spoken, some touch of the flesh. It did not come. Sutpen, who saw the importance of a family to his great scheme, failed to see what Stark Young's Hugh McGehee understood so perfectly: that the southern culture, the traditional code of ethics was to a certain extent a projection of family devotion, and once it was stripped of its basis in human affection it became worthless as a standard by which to live. Henry killed Bon, and Sutpen was deprived of his heir.

There is another book by Mr. Faulkner which demands consideration in any study of Civil War fiction. I refer to *The Unvanquished* which appeared in 1938. The main characters are the Sartorises, the point of view is that of Bayard, and the central theme, which receives partial development in each of the individual stories, is one of moral redemption through a modification of the inherited ethical order. As long as the formal conflict is in progress, the traditional southern morality is a responsible standard of conduct. It will serve to condone Granny's behavior when she steals mules, for she is working still for the public good, distributing money and stock to the poor. And it is sufficient, too, at the very end of the war, to suggest to Bayard and Ringo not only a general course of action, but also the specific *modus operandi* by which they track down and kill the bushwacker, Grumby. It remains perhaps a valid code even as late as 1866, when John Sartoris enters the polling booth with his derringer in his sleeve and shoots the two carpetbaggers named Burden. But from this point on, the code is doomed to fail; it will no longer furnish the basis for moral action. Once more the military defeat of the South coincides in time with a significant defection of the traditional ethic.

The old code is no longer adequate, because the time has finally come when even southern aristocrats like John Sartoris are no longer willing to live within the limits of the tradition. Sartoris builds a railroad. He launches his enterprise in partnership with Ben Redmond, and to the world of commerce he brings his fierce agrarian pride, his planter's code of honor. He must badger Redmond, abuse him, not because Redmond has been guilty of any breach of conduct, but because he, Sartoris, has attempted to operate in a strange world without altering the old ethic. Belatedly, he realizes his mistake, but by then, he must kill Redmond, who participates in the southern tradition, too, or he must, as happens, be killed by him. The responsibility for action is bequeathed to Bayard.

On the night of John Sartoris's murder, when Ringo is waiting to start the long ride back to Jefferson, Bayard pauses at the door to shake hands with Professor Wilkens.

I knew he believed he was touching flesh which might not be alive tomorrow night and I thought for a second how if I told him what I was going to do, since we had talked about it, about how if there was anything at all in the Book, anything of hope and peace for His blind and bewildered spawn which He had chosen above all others to offer immortality, *Thou shalt not kill* must be it, since maybe he even believed that he had taught it to me except that he had not, nobody had, not even myself since it went further than just having been learned. But I did not tell him. He was too old to be forced so, to condone even in principle such a decision; he was too old to have to stick to principle in the face of blood and raising and background, to be faced without warning and made to deliver like by a highwayman out of the dark: only the young could do that—one still young enough to have his youth supplied him gratis as a reason (not an excuse) for cowardice.

Bayard finds an answer. He does not reject the traditional morality: he modifies it, amalgamates it with the principles of Christianity.

Late in 1864, when the war is almost over, Charles Bon of *Absalom, Absalom!* speaks to Henry Sutpen. "Not God; evidently we have done without him for four years . . . and so if you don't have God you don't need food and clothes and shelter, there isn't anything for honor and pride to climb on and hold to and flourish. And if you haven't got honor and pride, then nothing matters."

Whether or not we have been doing without God ever since the war, I cannot say with any certainty. But even the spurious God, of whom Mr. Tate speaks, that diety fashioned by the sixteenth-century merchants, must have been sufficient for a while. Because in the Old South the honor and the pride were there, not as individual virtues in isolated men, but as a part of the public consciousness, the moral basis on which the culture was constructed. This is the reason the war has been used so often by so many southern writers. It is the grand image for the novelist, the period when the "ultimate truths," with which Mr. Faulkner says the writer must deal, existed as commonly recognized values within a social framework. It is the only moment in American history when a completely developed national ethic was brought to a dramatic crisis.

*Part Two*

# In Time of the
# Breaking of Nations:
# The Decline of
# Southern Fiction

It is, of course, too early to tell with any certainty what
has happened to the quality of southern fiction. There are
still plenty of southern writers around—more than ever
before. Taken as a whole, they are a remarkably gifted
group and they continue to publish novels and stories year
after year. They are not, however, as good as the brightest
stars of the previous generation. To cite only one example,
William Styron is a very competent novelist, but he cannot
be compared to Faulkner: or, if Faulkner is too stern a
comparison to make, Styron does not measure up to Robert
Penn Warren at his best.

This, I am aware, proves nothing. As students of literature have been telling themselves for the last twenty
years, the next truly great novel, the next general surge
of high-level creative activity may be just around the corner. Any day now, Cormac McCarthy or Madison Jones
or Elizabeth Spencer, or any one of a dozen or two other
novelists, might write the book that has the same enduring magnificence as a Faulkner novel or a Katherine Anne

Porter short story, and this might rekindle the renascence:
the finest flowering of all might be yet to come. But the
years pass and the new fruition has not developed, and
why it has not is a point worthy of our conjecture.

One conclusion to be drawn is that the present generation of writers, talented as it is, is not talented enough.
Styron and McCarthy and Spencer are simply not as gifted
as Faulkner and Warren and Lytle and the rest. The argument against accepting this answer is to be found in the
abrupt and very marked decline in the work of the already established writers after the close of World War II.
Consider Faulkner's career. Between 1929 and 1940, beginning with *Sartoris* and concluding with *The Hamlet*,
Faulkner published ten novels and two collections of short
stories, producing in both categories some of the best fiction ever written in this country. In 1942 he published
*Go Down, Moses*, which includes "The Bear." Then only
four years later came *Intruder in the Dust*, a bad book in
many ways and one somewhat unworthy of Faulkner's
genius. *Intruder in the Dust* was followed by four more
novels, all of them distinctly inferior. In 1948, when
Faulkner was fifty, his decline had set in.

Perhaps after his incredible thrust of creative endeavor
in the decade of the thirties, he had written himself out.
Perhaps his health was beginning to fail him; perhaps his
personal habits were interfering with his work. There are,
no doubt, any number of reasons why Faulkner's imagination might have gone stale and clumsy. But take, then,
the case of Warren, seven years younger than Faulkner,
who reached his zenith as a novelist in 1946 with the publication of *All the King's Men*. Since that time Warren has
written, in addition to poems and essays of various sorts,

five novels, each of which seems less satisfactory, less worthy of serious critical consideration than the one before. Caroline Gordon's best work was finished by 1945. *Ship of Fools*, Katherine Anne Porter's only new fiction in more than twenty years, was disappointing. Andrew Lytle has written one book in the last two decades. By 1946 all of Carson McCuller's major work except *The Ballad of the Sad Cafe* was finished, and Peter Taylor, skillful as he is, no longer shows us much that is new. Between 1925 and 1946 the southern literary renascence flourished: since that time the older writers have been no more successful than the young. And so, for the moment at least, the renascence is over.

There are many reasons why literary movements die. They use themselves up: they grow old as the impulses that bred them are fulfilled: and as they depict the material on which they feed, they consume their own sources. In the case of the southern renascence, while the process of natural maturation and subsequent decay went on, the social structure that fed the renascence was being modified by history. As everyone knows, the South between the two world wars was agrarian in its orientation; it had a sense of isolation from the rest of the country; it was conscious through its own experience of the tragic element in human history. Most important of all was its Protestant view of man, his nature, his condition on this earth, and his place in a definitely formulated eschatology. All values were derived from this Protestant source, and all the recurring images in southern literature draw their essential being from it. Whether or not the southern writer shared this viewpoint, whether he believed in any god at all, was of no consequence: it was there, a framework for

him to think and write within, a body of belief to be ma-
nipulated and dramatized and probed. And it freed him
from the necessity of explanation. Most first principles
were already accepted and defined. The writer did not have
to trouble himself with questions that great literature always treats as peripheral. In the best of Faulkner, none
of the characters asks himself, "Who am I?" They all know
who they are and even what they are: the question is what
they are going to do with their own virtue and sinfulness,
what qualities they will display in working out their fates,
what fortitude they will demonstrate in meeting their
destinies.

In the literature of the southern renascence, as in the
South of that time, man was seen as essentially mysterious. His beginning and the inception of his depravity were
crystallized in the mythology of *Genesis*. His end was
charted in the prophecy of *Revelation*. In between times,
he was himself a complex entity touched by everything
but elucidated by nothing: environment, heredity, experience, all went to shape him, but he was infinitely more than
the sum of his parts. At heart, man as he was viewed by
the writers of the renascence was an enigma. As such, he
was fit to play the roles he was asked to fill.

Today, in the South as elsewhere and in the minds of
southern writers, the generic image of man has been deprived of its mystery. Under the hegemony of the social
sciences, man is seen to be ultimately understandable, ultimately measureable, which means that in the end his behavior may be predicted and even controlled. No writer
escapes this view, and the one who embraces it necessarily
turns his attention from man himself, from the men and
women who are his people, from the sense of character

that has always been the *sine qua non* of good fiction, to
the social and political and economic reasons why. It is not
the character that we are interested in then, but the stimu-
lus which makes the character do what he does. Or to put
the matter another way, we find ourselves no longer moving from the concrete to the abstract, but vice versa. Our
thinking proceeds not from a man named Oedipus to a
theory about men who are in love with their mothers, but
in the opposite direction, from the theory—which may be
no more than that—to a character devised to fit the theoretical delineations.

However this may come out in the long run, and whatever the psychologists may finally learn that will help us
make out lives tranquil and happy, as of now, the best of
theories has not caught up with the simplest manifestation of ordinary humanity. Thus, man demystified is man
oversimplified, which is bad for art. It may not always
be wrong for the man of affairs to perceive the world in
terms of black and white. In the fourth section of "The
Bear," Ike McCaslin praises John Brown for having seen
the right and wrong of slavery in abecedarian terms, and
having acted on that vision without stopping to organize
committees or to indulge in agonizing second thoughts.
But John Brown was not a novelist, and the writer's first
job is to shade off the colors, to humanize the villain, and
to find the hero's flaw.

There are, I am sure, many reasons why the civil rights
struggle, fraught as it is with moral implications and inherent drama, has not yet furnished the material for a
really first-rate literary work. For one thing, we remain
too close to the events to get any sort of artistic perspective: even now the conflict continues, and the circum-

stances under which it is pursued alter as it enters each
new phase. But perhaps of more importance is the fact
that like writers everywhere, the southern writer today
finds himself deeply involved in the resolution of the social and political issues that beset his time. His loyalty is
divided between the call for direct action, direct participation in the affairs of the world on one hand and on the
other, his calling, his vocation to create sufficiently complex representations of life, to teach man about himself
through art. How this dilemma afflicted Yeats is common
knowledge. And while it is true that Stephen Crane and
Ernest Hemingway spent their lives in search of adventures which would test and be the sources of their fiction,
James was hostile to the cult of experience, and Joyce felt
it necessary to divest himself of all loyalties lest they drain
his emotional energy and inject a note of partisanship into
his work. To strive for justice is one thing: to be an artist
is quite another: and we are perhaps inclined to forget
occasionally how much devotion, how much total fidelity
great art requires.

Scholars often hold that one of the reasons the antebellum South produced no literature worthy of notice
was that all its creative impulses were dissipated in a defense of slavery. Now, in an ironic twist of history, many
southern writers—many more, I think, than is generally
known—use a good deal of their time and their strength
actively participating in the civil rights conflict. Many
others, while not actively engaged, are sympathetic to the
aims of the Negro revolution to the extent that their
thoughts and conversations tend to be less about literature and more and more about politics. What this will
mean to southern literature in the long run, I do not know:

but for the moment it means less time spent at the type-
writer; fewer books written; and quite possibly a reduced
level of competence for those whose forces must be divided between the demands of society and those of art.

For me, most significant of all is the sense I get from
southern writers and intellectuals in general that the civil
rights victory will be final, once it is won. There seems to
be a feeling, often expressed but even more often implied,
that when at last all the requirements for racial justice
have been fulfilled, life and man's estate therein will have
reached a happy stasis. This is a grave error to make, and
it is one that has damaged the southern writer's perceptions. If, contrary to all that history and literature have
taught us, we believe that any single mundane victory will
be absolute and enduring with no struggle to follow and no
future agony to endure, then we have lost touch with the
human condition, and we can, as novelists, no longer effectively tell the truth about the world. In the last scene
of *Hamlet*, while the dead bodies still surround him, For-
tinbras assumes the kingdom, his mind already vacillating
between what is over now and what is yet to come. The
final narrative chapter of *War and Peace* describes not an
end but a beginning: a new generation is growing toward
maturity: all is to start over, though the terms may be
different: all is to be gone through again. In his absolute
devotion to his cause, the southern writer has perhaps
forgotten this.

Finally, however much or little his work may have been
affected by his own relationship to social upheaval, whatever his own personal philosophy or the degree of his active commitment, the southern writer still must adjust his
thinking and his use of the images around him to the

ideological divisions of his age. It is a commonplace among historians and political scientists that the whole concept of nationalism is obsolete. Although much of the world has yet to learn this, it seems to me to be undeniably true, and a southern writer's failure to understand it will be reflected in his work. The time of the southern renascence was the time of political and social integrity of the southern nation, but now the southern nation is only a shell of its former self. Its physical characteristics have been changed by the growth of urban centers, the construction of super highways, and most of all by the innumerable products of the general postwar affluence in which the South has shared. The South is not the North; Atlanta is not New York; but neither Atlanta nor the South is at all what it used to be. The recent resurgence of segregationist sentiment is not so much a manifestation of southern contrariness as it is a facet of a larger social phenomenon which currently plagues the entire United States. As a group, Southerners may still be more conservative or more inclined toward religious belief than other people, but in being so, they identify themselves more and more with all those in other parts of the world who share their conservatism and their piety. Their loyalties transcend regional and national boundaries. Because this is true, southern images no longer mean what they used to mean; the concepts of southern history are changing; and whatever new myth can be created by southern novelists, we may be sure it will not be southern in the old sense.

Some of the attributes of the traditional South remain, and many of them are rich in drama. They can be used by the novelist: but they will have to be used. All the crazy characters in the South; all the sense of the past;

all the manners good and bad; all the woods and fields and
streams are only empty vessels now, and they will have to
be filled and reformed according to each individual writer's own metaphysic. And the southern writer had better
stop allowing himself to be misled. For the past twenty
years, young authors coming to maturity have congratu-
lated themselves on being born in Tennessee or Alabama
or Mississippi or Georgia, lands that they can both hate
and love, countries of rich tradition and tall tales. But the
self-praise was premature: living under the shadow of
the giants of the renascence and trying to follow in their
footsteps, the young writers have largely failed. The significant exception is Flannery O'Connor whose voice was
the only distinctly new and original one yet to arise in
the post-renascence South. Recently, a midwestern writer,
and a very good one, visited Nashville, which was his first
trip to the South since his early college days. He saw how
much and how little the South had changed since his last
visit, how much and how little it resembled the country
depicted in the novels and stories he had read. Finally, he
announced that he was now certain of what on his arrival
he had held only as a tentative judgment: that Flannery
O'Connor was a Catholic writer, not a southern writer
at all.

There is much truth in this conclusion: however southern she was, she was first a Catholic, and that made all
the difference. And if the southern renascence is to have a
new flowering, this is what the new generation of writers
must understand. The South, important as it still may be
as a ground of action, is no longer the prime mover, the
first principle on which a literary career may be built.
Like Flannery O'Connor, the new southern writer must

be something other than southern : his faith and his vision must be fixed somewhere beyond the southern experience : he must find his own source. Only then can he bring the old images alive once more.

# The New Faustus:
# The Southern Renascence and
# the Joycean Aesthetic

I want to begin with a brief discussion of two novels:
*An Exile* by Madison Jones and *The Confessions of Nat
Turner* by William Styron. *An Exile* is the story of Hank
Tawes, sheriff of a rural southern county, a man of reasonable competence and absolute honesty, whose worst
problem at the beginning of the book is a nagging wife.
In the course of the narrative, Tawes is seduced by the
daughter of a moonshiner, and thereby he becomes a party
to a violation of the law that he has sworn to uphold. Stern
consequences follow: Tawes's marriage breaks up, one of
his associates is killed as a result of his complicity, and,
in the end, though the murderous moonshiners are to be
brought to justice, Tawes pays with his life. The moral is
clear, and the book, like all of Jones's work, is full of bu-
colic imagery, of sequences flagrantly calculated to show
the evil of urbanization, and the questionable nature of
material progress. In many significant ways Jones is a
neo-Agrarian, and *An Exile* is a neo-Agrarian book.

Styron, like Jones, is a Southerner: both are the same

age, and both have published about the same amount of
work, but here the similarity between them seems to end,
Jones is a political conservative, Styron, a liberal. Jones's
prose is workmanlike, sometimes stolid, but always func-
tional and concrete. Styron is lyrical, his language is frequently beautiful, and he exhibits a tendency to overwrite.
To Jones the South is rural middle Tennessee, to Styron
it is Tidewater Virginia. Jones is Calvinist, Styron is existentialist, though neither is purely that; and superfi-
cially at least, *The Confessions of Nat Turner* and *An
Exile* are about as different as any two books could possibly be.

*Nat Turner* is, of course, the story of the slave insurrection of 1831, the events that led up to the bloodshed, the
executions that followed. But as Styron tells us in an introduction, *Nat Turner* is not so much an historical novel as
it is a "meditation on history" which perhaps accounts for
the book's episodic structure and its anachronistic tone.
The narrative follows Nat from his earliest memory to the
moment before his death: we are brought to see his relationships with various white owners and overseers: we
watch the development of his urgent need for vengeance—
or is it atonement, expiation, this terrible necessity for the
spilling of the white man's blood? We literally see the heads
roll, and after the carnage we wait with Nat in his cell,
listening to his final words, remembering, trying, along
with him, to discover why. Whether or not the book is successful, whatever we and those who follow us may think of
it ten or twenty or fifty or a hundred years from now, one
thing seems certain: Styron wrote with his eye on the
present and not on the past.

So this account, based on the history of more than a century ago, roots itself firmly in the here and now, and Jones's novel, which is contemporary, looks wistfully backwards, and in their distinctions and contradictions, the two novels would seem roughly to establish the limits within which all southern fiction is bound to fall. But a closer examination of the two works tends to demonstrate otherwise: it is my judgment that at their profoundest levels, *An Exile* and *Nat Turner* are expressions of a single hopelessness, a thrust toward destruction, the tired and jaded soul's longing for death.

Consider, in this light, the key scene in *An Exile*, the moment about which all the consequences of the narrative turn. When the sheriff stops an automobile for what begins as a routine investigation, the young driver abandons the vehicle leaving his female passenger to deal with the sheriff, and Tawes knows immediately what he has stumbled upon. The car is used for running moonshine, the tank under the back seat is doubtless full of whisky at this very moment; and the girl is more cheap than pretty, more forward than seductive: Jones draws her vividly in terms of tawdry hair ribbon and floral perfume. There is no earthly reason why the sheriff should be so taken with her that he would fail to do his duty. He has never seen her before, and his character has been established as that of a responsible, not a sensual or impulsive, man. Yet, in the twinkling of an eye, he abandons everything—duty, family, personal honor —and if Jones meant for us to infer that the sheriff's decision was a product of his lust, then the hero is not worthy of our sorrow, and the ensuing anger and agony do not signify.

But the girl is only a catalyst, a superficial reason that allows the sheriff to pursue a grim and deeper course. For

Tawes sees, as Jones does, that a general debauchery has
already overtaken the world. The landscape has been trans-
formed, the woods have been cut, the streams have been
defiled, and the air has been polluted. Traditional values
have been ridiculed into desuetude, religion has been
stripped of its mysteries by modern theology, and both
public and private institutions have fallen into decay. What
the sheriff seeks within this frame is not success or honesty
or sexual fulfillment or even the exercise of charity, but
rather the peace that follows upon self-destruction. He
wants out of a world that has been turned hideous by its
loss of a sense of moral values, and the girl is his oppor-
tunity: she furnishes him the means. With intractable
purpose, Tawes strips himself of the old loyalties which
might deter him: he seeks guilt as a gentler soul might
gather flowers, and thereby motivates and accrues significance for his own end. In Madison Jones's canon, Tawes
is no exception: this is the way Jones sees the plight of
modern man.

And so it is with Styron. Nat Turner lives in another
time and works out his destiny under a vastly different set
of circumstances and presents to us a face of another color,
but he and Sheriff Tawes are nonetheless brothers under
the skin. As is the case with Tawes, on the surface what
Turner is and what Turner ultimately does will not jibe.
As Styron draws him for us, Nat Turner is intelligent, perceptive, capable, consumed with hatred for white people,
but kind and loyal to his Negro friends. He survives and
even thrives under certain of his masters because he is not
only a mechanic of great skill, an inventor, and therefore
a valuable property, but he is a master of human relations,
a shrewd psychologist who knows how to deal with his op-

pressors, an accomplished dissembler who possesses monumental self-control. He is an idealization rather than a realistic portrayal, an exaggerated composite of many splendid human qualities, and as such, he jars violently against what Styron finally has him do. I do not mean that I find his hate for his masters unmotivated or that one would not expect him, sooner or later, to shed white blood. But the insurrection had no hope of success, and whatever the real Nat Turner might have foreseen in this connection, Styron's Nat Turner would have had to know from the outset that what he planned was doom. Perhaps it can be argued that his willingness to sacrifice his friends was evidence of his heroic stature, that only a figure of tragic proportions would see the necessity for leading those he loved to a bloodletting that was bound to terminate in their own deaths. But this is not the point I wish to make or to refute.

It is germane to my interpretation of the novel that once the insurrection has started, Turner finds himself unable to kill. His axe will not strike the flesh toward which he directs it: his muscles will not move to destroy at his brain's command. The single murder that he is able to perpetrate is that of Margaret Whitehead, and this is not vengeance at all, but an act of love. He is leaving a world which has grown unworthy for human habitation, and he will take her with him, and it is she whom he thinks about later just before he dies. What we are dealing with, then, is not the old Nat Turner of our shameful history, but a new creation, a man with a voice that is insistently modern and therefore insistently hopeless: he is one with the *personae* in the plays of LeRoi Jones: his spirit is that of Stokely Carmichael and Rap Brown. In a world too far depraved to be reformed, he has given up all expectation of being delivered from oppression: he desires now only to destroy and to be destroyed. On these terms, the novel makes sense. And on these terms, Madison Jones and William Styron, Sheriff Tawes and Nat Turner meet, though they began their journeys at opposite poles. In a faithless universe, all our heroes wish for death. Why should this be? How did our literature, and by inference our society, come to this?

In an effort to shed some light on those questions, I want to turn to James Joyce, not to *Ulysses*, which has had such an extravagant influence on the twentieth-century novel, but to *A Portrait of the Artist as a Young Man*, which seems to me to be partly a prophecy of what we as people and as writers are becoming and partly a description of what we have already become. *A Portrait* has been too widely read to require recapitulation. As everyone knows, it is the story of young Stephen Dedalus, which is to say, James Joyce, who grows up, goes to school, reads, writes, sins, repents, considers becoming a priest, and finally, in the climactic epiphany scene, discovers that his destiny is to follow his mythical namesake, to become a maker, a writer, and, as he puts it, "to recreate life out of life!"

Now, *A Portrait* has a very curious structure. Since the time of Jane Austen, almost all novels have been built according to the same general pattern. The first two-thirds or three-quarters of the narrative are devoted to an introduction of the characters and the elements of the plot, a statement of theme, and a development of all these to a point of maximum complication. Here the story begins its run toward its conclusion: dramatic tension increases as the plot unwinds: the writer's style tightens up, and though he may put in a hold here and there to keep his momentum from carrying him too rapidly toward the end, the time for digressions and the introduction of new material—not to mention philosophizing—is soon over.

In *A Portrait*, the epiphany scene occurs almost exactly two-thirds of the way through the novel. It is a climax, a peak of Stephen's spiritual life, and therefore the reader would ordinarily expect the narrative to turn here and to start toward its denouement. But the opposite takes place: there follow a number of conversations between Stephen and members of his family, Davin, the dean, a group of students, Lynch, Cranly. The old rejections, which are the meat of the first two-thirds of the book, are taken up once more. Stephen will not learn Gaelic, or join the Irish revolutionary party, or sign the Tsar's petition for universal peace. Finally, there is a discussion of aesthetic theory before the story reaches the highly dramatic material of Stephen's total rejection of the Church.

What this unusual structure proves first of all is that there are no absolute rules which writers must follow: one can do anything if he is good enough and Joyce was. But beyond this, there is the question of emphasis, of whether, given the novel's construction, our primary concern should be with Stephen's discovering that he wants to be an artist, or rather with his determination, once he has made this discovery, that he will achieve competence, that he will gain skill at whatever cost. There is, I think, a tendency on the part of modern readers to see in *A Portrait* what we take to be a natural and largely unmitigable relationship of epiphany and exile. We assume that, since Stephen wants to be a writer, it is therefore imperative that he free his mind and his temperament from all feeling and thought that are

not purely artistic. He must abandon his family and leave
Ireland to keep from being annoyed by them, to preserve
himself from the demands they might make on his time
and energy. He is, we think, right to break with the Church,
right to fear "the chemical action which would be set up in
his soul by a false homage to a symbol behind which we are
massed twenty centuries of authority and veneration." We
conceive his only duty, his only loyalty to be to his art, and
in seeing him in this way, we do not deviate greatly from
the world's conventional concept of the generic artist.

But a closer reading of *A Portrait* and particularly a
more attentive examination of its structure might lead us
to another conclusion. Joseph Frank and others have
shown how modern novelists manipulate form in order to
bring the various parts of their narratives into more meaningful juxtapositions. Where scenes are placed in a novel,
how the novel is put together are very important indeed,
and it was neither chance nor ignorance that induced
Joyce to place his discussion of aesthetics where the reader
would expect to find a passage of dramatic action, nor was
he careless in throwing repeated emphasis on Stephen's
rejection of religion and in using this rejection as the ultimate climax of the book. My point is that a proper interpretation of the novel must see the rejections not as ordinary and predictable consequences of an artistic ambition,
but as free choices consciously selected and deliberately
made. Ever solicitous of the role he plays, Stephen strikes
a pose of Satanic majesty. "I will not serve," he tells
Cranly, echoing Lucifer. And though he no longer believes,
he does not completely disbelieve, and he is prepared to pay
the terrible price that his apostasy might exact. "I will tell
you also what I do not fear," he says. "I am not afraid to

make a mistake, even a great mistake, a lifelong mistake and perhaps as long as eternity too." For the sake of his art and his competence therein, he will risk damnation.

It would be going too far to say that *A Portrait* is a twentieth-century version of the Faustus legend. I know of no evidence that Joyce intended any such thing, but the parallels between the old necromancer and the young Dedalus are sufficiently striking not to be ignored. Faustus—I think now of Marlowe's traditional version—traded his soul to the devil for a power that he found himself increasingly unable to use properly. The story, as its continuing appeal to writers of all sorts attests, has many facets. It is a monument to the vanity of man, it is indicative of man's demonic proclivities: and the playing out of the narrative invariably involves an assault upon established order, both transcendent and mundane. One of the remarkable aspects of *A Portrait* is the manner in which Joyce is able to develop Stephen's pride to the point that it becomes a dynamic force in the book. Like Faustus, he considers himself spiritually and intellectully superior to the common run of humanity, and it is this phase of his character, not weakness of the flesh or his talents and competencies, that furnishes the basic motivations for the drama and makes the novel work. To be sure, in the strict sense, Stephen, unlike Faustus, has no direct commerce with the devil, and, indeed, he thinks probably that the devil does not exist. But should he exist, Stephen has delivered himself knowingly into his hands. Finally, and most significantly, for the sake of increased literary power, i.e., his own kind of magic, Stephen abandons the sources of political and social and metaphysical order with results in many ways similar to those that Faustus achieved.

At the beginning of Marlowe's play, when Faustus is first succumbing to the temptations of his own vanity, he casts himself in the role of benefactor of mankind. He will change the landscape, alter political structures, and otherwise alleviate the problems of the human state. But the course of his use of power is one long decline, and he is reduced finally to the perpetration of empty exhibitions and practical jokes. In the general dissipation of his morality, he becomes petty, vindictive, dishonest. At the last, he is insensitive to the suffering he once meant to assuage, and the power for which he traded his soul has grown maleficent in his hands. It will be considered literary heresy, I know, but I submit that something of the same thing happened to Joyce.

*A Portrait* ends at just exactly the right place. The great rejections have been made: the full weight of them, what they mean, what they imply is clear: Stephen's courage in setting out on his own is gloriously realized. But Stephen and Joyce go on, Stephen into *Ulysses*, Joyce to the remaining days and years of his life, all of them devoted to, revolving totally around, his own literary ambition. It is, of course, a risky business to equate what is made with the maker, the character with the author, but in this case, the risk is well taken: Joyce is Stephen: Stephen is Joyce. It is also true that the character of Stephen in *Ulysses* amends, in certain particulars, the Stephen of *A Portrait*. And Joyce insisted that the word *Young* was the key to his title, thus implying that both he and Stephen had subsequently changed. Unquestionably they did, but the rejections remained inviolate. Joyce was almost symbolically tardy in regularizing his relationship with Nora, his animosity toward Ireland continued unabated, and he died beyond the sacraments of the Church.

All of this is important to us for a number of reasons. First, the power Joyce dealt for in his rejection of the sources of order served him no better than, in an earlier day, it had served Faustus. From the magnificence of his previous achievement, particularly in "The Dead" and in *A Portrait* itself, Joyce's subsequent career was a decline through largely empty experimentation into what for all practical purposes can only be called the meaninglessness of *Finnegans Wake*. I am aware, as I have already indicated, of the great influence that *Ulysses* has exerted on the form of the novel. Its authority is everywhere to be felt. No one works outside its vast hegemony. But influence is one thing and accomplishment is something else. Often they are coincident: as often they are not: in art, as in science, the pioneer will not necessarily produce the finished product. I do not think *Ulysses* is a good book. It is intellectually a masterpiece: it is fraught with breathtaking stylistic accomplishments. But it is an empty novel. In spite of all its truly impressive technique, it has no moral center. The Molly Bloom soliloquy, celebrated as it is, is tantamount to Faustus' plucking fruit in the dead of winter.

There would be nothing to fear from all this, if we, like Marlowe's audiences, saw Faustus not only as tragic protagonist, but as a cautionary figure, a warning of what will happen to us if we follow in his footsteps. But on the contrary, two generations of artists and intellectuals have seen Stephen Dedalus solely as hero, and they have viewed his rejections as elements in a legitimate quest for artistic freedom which should be emulated by all. On the campus,

in publishing houses, in workshops and symposia and the-
aters and libraries, Stephen Dedalus has become our folk
hero. Which is to say, in the modern literary community,
Faustus has become Everyman. We, too, have abandoned
all loyalty to family, state, and the substantive forms of religion. We have even taken the next logical step: the active
pursuit of disorder has become an end to the extent that we
perpetrate revolt on almost every level, not for a redress of
real grievances, but for the sake of establishing the an-
archy that has become our goal. We interdict our mental
processes by drugs; we acknowledge the meaningless
mouthing of any hairy exhibitionist to be legitimate poetry,
as Philip Rahv has pointed out, we choose our saints from
the ranks of moral idiots such as Jean Genet. Our novelists
write of antiheroes—disorder again—who live by the premise that there is no such thing as right and wrong. Or
take the case of William Burroughs. Not content with the
confusion that is native to his obscene tracts, he shuffles his
pages and jumbles his lines after his manuscripts are finished, and he is praised by Norman Mailer and Mary Mc-
Carthy and hundreds of others who ought to know better
for the beauty and—mark the word—the *freedom* he has
brought to art. We try to salve our consciences by violent
partisanship and a staunch devotion to selected and intellectually popular causes, but by any measure that is appli-
cable, we continue in our spiritual and ethical decline.

And we shall not be saved by our enhanced literary competence. Technique and style are not sufficient: words, no
matter how beautifully they are put together, are not
enough. But in many cases, words are all we have, and thus
we witness a new school of literary endeavor: the novel
about the novel, or about style, or about language, or mean-

ing, or the novel that is a burlesque of itself. This is literature that ceases to signify in any recognizable sense, and
which degenerates into elaborate connundrums and extended puns. This is what Joyce predicted and in a way
made possible for us. And it is against this background that
I should like to examine the southern renascence.

The reasons that are usually given for the flowering of
southern literature in the decades following World War I
are sufficiently familiar to us now that we need not dwell on
them. We are told that the South was a homogenous society: that it knew the meaning of defeat and suffering,
having lost the Civil War: that it was agrarian in its basic
orientation and therefore in tune with nature and with the
particular view of reality that a knowledge of and depen-
dence on the seasons is likely to impose. Southern society
was said to be religious—or more specifically, Protestant—
conservative, and blessed with the ability, according to
Richard Weaver, to understand that the whole of a thing
was greater than the sum of its parts. The South was im-
poverished and cursed with a class system—the Negro at
the bottom—which may or may not have been a good thing
for literature, depending on which critic you prefer. The
Southerner saw the world and its history as a series of images, rather than as a sweep of theories, which is to say
that his vision was not abstract, but concrete. And finally,
for my summation, the southern artist saw that the traditional society in which he lived and about which he wrote
was on the verge of dissolution: he struck his chronicle of
it in the twilight of its going.

I suppose at this point it is hardly necessary for me to
say that although I recognize and even urge the validity of

all the foregoing reasons for the renascence, it is the last—
should I call it the *Götterdämmerung* theory?—which most
appeals to me. I know the dangers of substantive criticism:
I am fully aware, I think, that if we begin to judge literature by the attitudes it reflects, by what it says, rather than
how it says it, we are opening a Pandora's box of frighten-
ing dimensions. We are exposing ourselves to a score of
illegitimate ideological claims and romantic excesses. But
there is no easy or absolute way to assess literary merit.
There is no critical method which does not involve risk. An
evaluation of the theme, along with the moral outlook, the
world view, the metaphysical view from which the author
writes, is ultimately necessary. There are many books tech-
nically more perfect than *War and Peace* and *Don Quixote. A Portrait of the Artist as a Young Man* is one of them.
But who would dare say that *A Portrait* is on the same
plane with these two masterpieces?

So I see the set of values which prevailed in the South
during the twenties and thirties as at least a *sine qua non*,
if not the major source of the literary renascence. Other
American writers, from other sections of the country, were
also writing well, and it is not mere coincidence that the
best of them were dealing with the decline of accustomed
belief: Hemingway in *The Sun Also Rises* and *A Farewell
to Arms*, Fitzgerald in *The Great Gatsby*, Dos Passos in
*U.S.A.*, and there were others. But in the South the traditional society with its traditional values was more fully
intact, and because the South had been isolated for the previous half century or more, its confrontation with the postwar disillusionment was more dramatic. This, along with
the other characteristics and circumstances which have

been set forth, was the ground out of which the original renascence developed.

Now, the old society with its old views is, if not dead, so far weakened that it is no longer viable in a literary sense. The southern outlook is no longer agrarian: Southerners as a whole are no longer pious or respectful of tradition: and the fabric of southern life—which now is largely bourgeois life—changes every day. And the South has suffered the common alienation. Unlike Faulkner, who during the thirties hunted and fished and drank with a cross-section of the people in and around Oxford, the typical contemporary southern artist is so far divorced in attitude and temperament from the ordinary citizen that the two cannot meet without falling out: and frequently the southern artist eschews southern society totally and goes to live in a more congenial place such as Roxbury, Connecticut. Finally, the southern writer or intellectual is as conformist in his ethical and aesthetic dispositions as the artists and intellectuals of New York or California or New Mexico.

It is my judgment that the novels and poems being written today, in the South as elsewhere, are not as good as those which were written in the twenties and thirties. I do not think they are apt to be as good until we are able to bring ourselves to a new iconoclasm. We must, somehow, destroy the notions that order is bad, that technique is all, that aesthetics furnish a sufficient code of life, and that picketing the courthouses or the corner café are the sole requisites for ethical fulfillment. This is not to say, as I doubtless will be accused of saying, that we must turn back. We cannot turn back any more than we can raise the dead or stop the sun or part the ocean. We are where we

are in history and the past is past : nor can we pretend that
the old society exists or that we are products of it. We will
have to find our own way out. As individual writers, we will
have to discover our own sources of moral organization.

Which is what Flannery O'Connor did. She brought to
the old southern images her strict devotion to her Roman
Catholic God and her fully developed sense of a universe
which operates under the terms of His provenance. The
social disintegrations that she portrayed in her books are
all measured against her sense of good and evil. Her fiction
was full of her knowledge of the destiny of man according
to Christian eschatology. And in her best work, the clash of
angelic and demonic forces is clearly present. Therefore,
when Tarwater baptizes the retarded child Bishop and
drowns him in the process, we are dealing with something
more than mere southern grotesque : the scene achieves a
significance that extends, without mimicking, the last
pages of *The Sound and the Fury*.

Thus Flannery O'Connor has shown us one way to make
what remains of the southern experience and landscape the
vital literary materials that they used to be. There are
doubtless other paths back toward a sense of morality and
the stability of order. But for the moment, at least, I do not
think they are likely to be social. I do not conceive of finding in the near future a sufficient authority in the image of
the family or the image of the state or in the images of the
organizations and movements to which we pledge our loyalties, the frame of regularity within which we can work out
the deviations which are our art. I do not say that in order
to write we must all become Roman Catholics. But we must
become *something* : we must see the world as larger than

ourselves or our generation or our ability to send a space
ship to the moon.

And I am finally optimistic: I believe that beyond this
present lull in the renascence there is the possibility of re-
newed fruition. Perhaps in spite of what we have done to
ourselves and to our environment, we in the South, alone of
all people, have by virtue of God's grace or by Malthusian
accident, enough remaining of what went into the old renascence to furnish material to the themes and impulses
of the new. We shall never again be agrarian. But our cities
will never be as large as New York or Los Angeles. And
because we have come to them later and under different circumstances, we see the urban experience in a different
light. We have left to us something of the old sense of character, which is to say we continue to view people as individuals, and our gifts for narrative and for taking the concrete view are not totally dead. They await our rediscovery.
But we must continue to remind ourselves that this will not
occur as a result of some general enlightenment. In terms
of mundane history, each of us is alone to an extent that
even Joyce never dreamed of. And each of us will have to
escape the new Faustus in his own way.

# Southern Writers in
# the Modern World:
# Death by Melancholy

I should like to start by stating a few assumptions which, if they are not self-evident, have at least been so thoroughly discussed as to require no further elaboration. First: that the southern literary renascence ended in the mid-forties with the termination of World War II; that no writing done since then has measured up to that done before; that we have now no novelist as good as Faulkner, no poets as good as Ransom or Tate; and that Faulkner himself was not as good after the war as he was before it. His major phase ended with "The Bear" in 1942, and except for a few isolated works such as *All the King's Men* and "Seasons of the Soul," the renascence was at that moment effectively over.

My second assumption is that the renascence did not die because of a dearth of talent. While it is probably true that Faulkner was the kind of genius who appears once in a century, the last twenty years have nonetheless seen the coming of age of an extraordinary number of young Southerners who are generously gifted. Their names come immediately to mind : William Styron, Madison Jones, Flannery O'Connor, Cormac McCarthy, James Dickey, and many, many others. Some of these—Styron and McCarthy in particular—wrote better first books than most of their distinguished predecessors, and yet in no case have the promising beginnings of the younger writers been fulfilled. They have dribbled away into repetition and mediocrity, but the firm talent shining through these efforts is easily to be seen.

Therefore, and I do not know whether this is a third assumption or merely a completion of the second, it seems apparent that a part of our present difficulty is to be found in the age. We know from our study of literature that some ages have been better than others for writers. Shakespeare was the rarest of geniuses, but the whole Elizabethan period cannot be explained in terms of genetic accident: it was not a matter of a largesse of talent being distributed from heaven. The culture helped. There was something in the air. Then as time passed, the flower faded. The Cromwellian interregnum came, and all was changed, never to be the same again. My contention is that something of this sort happened in the American South.

Now, if what I have said so far is true, then the next assumption indisputably follows: if we are going to write well in and about the present time, we must understand that our world is different from that of the twenties and thirties, and therefore we will have to look at it through our own eyes and find our own ways to write about it. To paraphrase C. Vann Woodward, we must shake off the burden of southern literature. We cannot forget Faulkner : we must not under any circumstances stop reading him : but we must stop trying to write in his fashion, and we must above all come to a new understanding of the culture that

produced the renascence and the ways in which it is different from ours.

Up to now, it has been our custom, and rightly so, following some of the most perceptive critics of our time, to
think of the South in which the southern renascence was
rooted largely in terms of its agrarian delineations. The
people, being farmers, had lost the Civil War, and therefore
they knew about the tragedy of life: living close to the land,
they understood the inscrutable quality of providence.
Dealing with mules and boll weevils rather than with
stocks and bonds, they had a firmer grasp of reality than
their city counterparts. And so the argument went and
goes, its ramifications developed to include the class structure and the piety of the populace. All of this is accurate
and it will serve to explain the place of the South in American history and to elucidate the renascence as a phenomenon of our national literature. And I do not minimize the
importance of the agrarian background. The novel, particularly, is founded in the concrete and mundane aspects
of a culture. In many meaningful ways, the details of the
life that is depicted are the essence of the novel, and except
in rare cases every author is exceedingly anxious to be absolutely accurate in his rendering of costume and custom,
of time and place. But the physical details of the culture
are not final in the shaping of the literary work. What is
ultimate is what Conrad—using a felicitous word—called
the *temperament* of the artist: that is his mind and his
heart, his sense of the universe and of himself in it, all that
vast complex of beliefs and impulses and perceptions that
make him what he essentially is.

Of course, temperament, too, is a product of culture. Or

rather, temperament is the *first* product of culture, though not, indeed, the child of environment alone: certainly the chromosomes work their function. But the mold within which the inherent gift will shape itself is cast by the glories and exigencies of time and place, before a line is written or a literary idea takes shape. And because it is the prime mover, the temperament—which is the way of seeing, the analytical and formulating and recognizing and reacting part—the temperament is, in a manner of speaking, everything. It is the mysterious well from which creativity flows, and its thrusts and judgments dictate all that follows: the words, the style, the structure, the technique.

It is a paradox—and literary endeavor, like life, is full of paradoxes—that the temperament which is shaped by the environment that has bred it must assume a totally ambiguous position *vis-a-vis* the society in which it exists. Here again, we see what has been up until our own immediate time, a common posture of the artist, differentiated largely only in terms of degree. The writer is of his time and not of his time, he is a citizen of his country and not a citizen of his country. As one author of my acquaintance has put it, one must feel about his culture the same way he feels about his mother: he loves her deeply, but she does many things which annoy him and some things of which he profoundly disapproves. It is the familiar love-hate relationship that Dickens had for London, that Faulkner had for Mississippi, that resulted finally in Tolstoy—that truly pious man—being excommunicated from the Russian Church. Since the Middle Ages, the artist has been always more or less alienated, and as century succeeded century, the pattern became increasingly one of more alienation than less. Again somewhat paradoxically, the artist was supported and even vindicated in his alienation by the society he opposed.

I want to make clear that I am not thinking now of the ordinary mistrust that exists between the tradesman and the artist, or of works such as *Bleak House* and *The Grapes of Wrath*, which attack one or another aspect of the body politic, or even of the struggles that developed between men such as James Joyce and D. H. Lawrence and the appointed or self-appointed guardians of public morals. What I am seeking to describe is that pattern of tension that developed between heretical, agnostic, or atheistic writers and the Christian society in which they worked and lived. This was important for many reasons. In the first place, we must remember—or more than that, in our present circumstances we must continue to remind ourselves—that at least for the last two thousand years all our literature has been Christian in a broad sense: no matter how iconoclastic it might have been, it has participated in the prevailing Christian culture. It has depicted people living in societies that to a greater or less extent held Christian beliefs and values, and therefore Christian theology furnished the standard against which all acts of morality and all concepts of being were finally measured. If the writer were a Christian, he was able to pursue his artistic ends in terms of the discrepancy between the ideal of human conduct founded on charity, and life as man actually lives it. But it was of no consequence that the writer might be and often was of another religion or of none at all. He still operated within a social structure composed of people who largely acceded to a common frame of belief. Whether or not he shared the faith, he made artistic use of the symbols and the narratives and the ethical standards which generated from the commonly held religious view.

Curiously, even through the declining years of the Christian hegemony, the decaying Christian society was able to maintain the writer, to furnish a world for him to write about and to sustain him in whatever tensions he projected within that world. For his part, the writer, indulging himself in the seriousness with which he approached and practiced his vocation, turned his fidelity and his piety away from God and lavished it on his craft. Indeed, what I am attempting to describe here has been codified for us: Joyce shows it all with exquisite skill in *A Portrait of the Artist as a Young Man*. I have already said, on another occasion, that in my judgment, Stephen Dedalus—not Thomas Mann's Adrian Leverkuhn—is the real twentieth-century Faustus, though in many respects, the two are very much alike. However, Dedalus was a believer in a sense that Leverkuhn never was, and he opted for mortal beauty rather than eternal love by echoing the words of Lucifer—"I will not serve"—but without extracting a firm promise from the Prince of Darkness. He relinquished belief, charity, the proper appetites of the will in order to enhance his creative gift, which was his own kind of magic. This choice was Joyce's, as well as Stephen's, and what Joyce later did with the skill that he purchased so dearly, I need not now go into. But working strictly in Scholastic terms, he furnished for the intellectuals of our age a new theology.

Aquinas, discovering his pattern in the Christian Trinity, sets forth three qualities that are required for beauty, which Joyce translates from the Latin, quite conventionally, as wholeness, harmony, and radiance. These are all familiar to us, and the first two are easily grasped. Whole-

ness is understood as our apprehension of the work of art
as a single thing, an entity limited and separate from all
the other things that are in the world. Harmony exists in
the relationship of the parts of this thing which we have
established as one, the pleasing arrangement of these parts
seen in terms of their various juxtapositions to each other.
So far so good, and to his point, Joyce and Aquinas proceed
in agreement. But there remains radiance, the *claritas* of
the original: this Aquinas sees as the essence of Being,
which comes from and is God. For Joyce, radiance is the
artistic rendition of the moment of epiphany. The artist,
making use of his heightened perceptions, has seen and
recognized in the common fabric of life some instant of in-
effable significance and beauty. The recapturing of this experience in its bright coloration is the source of radiance.

The consequences of Joyce's defection are too vast and
numerous even to be listed here. I wish to point out only
that the source of beauty has been changed from God to
man, and with this shift has come a new concept of the
nature of the act of creation. The Christian, the Jew, the
Muslim, the Buddhist—all who cling to a divine faith or
embrace a transcendent vision know that the only Creator
is God. Man does not create. He rearranges, he makes
choices, but these arrangements and choices simply effect
new uses of material that already exists. So art is a means
of discovery and disclosure, an act of secondary creativity
that yearns toward a revelation of Being, *claritas*. The
writer who understands his art in these terms still finds
his life to be ruled by his artistic gift: he is the dedicated
and unflagging servant of his work. But like Thomas More,
he is God's servant first.

Such a state, such a frame of mind and reference on the

part of the artist, such a fidelity to his Creator as I am trying here to describe are so rarely seen or explicated in our
time as to be all but incomprehensible to modern man. The
Joyce-Dedalus-Faustus camp has so far carried the day
that when one speaks of a religious attitude toward art, he
is likely to be understood as recommending that poems and
novels be written solely on theological or clerical or hagio-
logical subjects. There is nothing wrong with such subjects, but the use of them is beside the point. More germane
is Conrad's claim, which I referred to earlier, that all art
is an appeal of the individual temperament of the artist to
all the other temperaments which will apprehend the work.
Which is another way of saying, the work is the artist, the
artist is the work. Therefore, the man who practices his
faith, with all that this entails, and who sees his craft in its
relationship to God's being—this man will write a different
kind of love or adventure story than the man who believes
that art itself is a primary pursuit and an ultimate end.

The great master of our time, Faulkner himself, was an
example of the latter type. Recall his reply to the inter-
viewer from the *Paris Review*. "The Writer's only responsibility is to his art. . . . If a writer has to rob his mother,
he will not hesitate; the 'Ode on a Grecian Urn' is worth
any number of old ladies." On a lower level, this statement
develops the same sort of fallacy that prompted Stephen
Dedalus to reject God. The Irishman and the Southerner
share a false dichotomy: the belief that we cannot have
both God and art or probity and art; and the willingness
acted out or at least expressed in advance to abandon God
or probity or both on the chance that they might interfere
with the artist's exalted calling. Such an abandonment of
metaphysical reality changes the artist radically and radi-

cally alters the nature of his art. Nonetheless, for a long
time, this was an attitude that worked for the writer amaz-
ingly well.

The artist was able to go his own way, worshipping his
trade above all else because like a great and imperfect
guardian angel, society shaped the culture and determined
the circumstances, mundane and otherwise, under which
the writer worked. As I have already said, insofar as the
society was Christian, the writer wrote about a Christian
society, for there is nothing else to write about except the
life that the writer sees and knows. Insofar as the society
maintained its respect for, if not its practice of, morality,
this morality was reflected in the writer's work. But what
happens to the artist and his art when the fundamental nature of society changes? When, as has now occurred, the
level of Christian ritual and practice is reduced below the
point where it exercises any primary influence in the affairs of men? Or to state it more simply, what is the result
when the secular artist has brought the culture at large
around to his way of thinking?

As the world empties, its metaphysical concepts drain-
ing away, charity growing more and more scarce, and even
that imperfect habit of love that lingers after charity is
gone, falling into desuetude—as the moral ardor of the
world cools, the artist is thrust back upon his own re-
sources. He must look to himself while all around him the
conditions of life deteriorate. Once God is rejected and the
divine affections are thereby stifled, the other affections
are also stunted and distorted. The Christian virtues such
as chastity and obedience are put aside; rational goods
such as honor and courage and love of tranquility—all the
qualities that were so important in Faulkner's major work

and which he named in his Nobel prize speech—are called into question; and in extreme cases, in those areas of the world where God in all His manifestations has truly been abandoned, even the natural affection for the simple necessities of life and the good health that they produce has been abrogated. The writer finds himself bereft of a moral frame within which to develop his characters and work out his plots. There is no place to start, there are no standards by which people and actions can be judged: in a meaningless world there is no way to develop meaning. So the writer looks within himself and finds there only an equal emptiness.

Or rather, he finds art itself, art long worshipped for the sake of method, art based not on the Being of God, but on the epiphany of the artist. Believing in nothing beyond himself, knowing nothing in the proper sense—for mundane knowledge, uninformed by a sense of metaphysical truth is fragmentary and distorted—the writer finds his genius mysteriously blighted. He continues to try to work, but his range has narrowed. He can write about art itself, and he has and he does, but with less and less success, for writing about writing as such descends before long into a technical exercise informed by nothing more substantial than self-adulation. Or he can try to cling to what remains of decency in life by poking among the moral ashes, left cold and gray by the rejection of the mystery. That is, he can seek his theme in the secular morality of the day, in whatever social problem commands our attention—the race question, the peace movement—and in terms of which alone, out of all the possibilities of human conduct, we measure our worth and dignity and generosity as men, for so long as that particular issue is popular. Which is to say,

we pursue individual ethical goals separately and for themselves alone, with no consideration of their ontological
context. Or the artist can decide to build a new world to
write about, thus rejecting at once all the wisdom of the
ages, all the standards and beliefs by which men have lived
for millennia, all the revealed and discovered truths that
we are properly heir to.

Or he can repeat the past, writing poorly for a second or
third time what has already been written well. But which-
ever of these solutions he may choose, the result will be the
same: at worst, chaos and literary charlatanism: at best,
good, honest writing that is frequently skillful, but which
cannot hide the hollowness at the core. As writers and critics and readers, we try to fool ourselves. We speak of our
new way of doing things as if failure were to be excused
because of its novelty or as if novelty itself were proof of
virtue. We give each other good reviews and demand of
each other less and less in the way of good characterization,
sensible structure, maturity of theme. But we do not fool
ourselves: we truly know that nothing comes of nothing:
and though we do not admit it, we are aware of the emptiness of our corporate existence and the bleakness of our
individual souls.

As writers, we have fallen victim to our own excesses,
and a deep melancholy now grips our lives. We see that our
new god, art, has failed us: that no matter how absolute
our devotion is to our trade, no matter how hard we work
or how diligently we pursue our craft, no matter how fran-
tically we search for new existential or technical solutions,
the result is the same. Our books remain purposeless and
tawdry. Our efforts fail; our false faith shatters against
reality; and our belief in art as method, art as ego, issues

into a hidden wish for our own demise. For how else, except in terms of our desire for self-destruction, our quest for the death of the spirit which is the true and only death —in what other way can we explain our ineffectual obsession with the flesh?

Having killed the soul, we cherish the body and seek its salvation, for we have nothing else left to try to save. For us, sex is the final good, physical death is nemesis, and according to this new duality, we order our lives. People of all ages subscribe to the cult of youth because to be young is to be strong in sexual prowess and—if the actuarial tables are to be believed—far from death. But the sex that we seek in our lives and in our books is unsatisfactory; for just as our separation from God who is Being has vitiated our quintessential reality, so our rejection of God who is Love has wrought an incapacity of the heart. This is reflected in our work. In our search for meaning, or what we are more likely to call relevance, we chronicle not only the minute details of sexual relationships between more or less ordinary men and women, but the adventures of homosexuals, sado-masochists, and necromaniacs as well. Since both the artist and the society in which he works have dissipated their powers of distinction, the more simpleminded and depraved a work is, the more apt we are to hail it as a magnificent achievement—as is attested by the fame of such antimoralists as Henry Miller and Jean Genet and William Burroughs.

Or, we take seriously *Catch 22* and *Dr. Strangelove*, because our loftiest theme is the sacredness of mere physical life—to be lived preferably with the organs intact, but to be lived: all can be forgiven modern man except the act of dying. But the mere life of the body is not life at all, and

existence pursued beyond the reach of being's proper
source fades into ennui and deep sadness. It is out of boredom that we keep searching for new physical sensations,
new sexual deviations, new drug experiences which are
celebrated as positive goods in the books we write. It is
sorrow that makes us protest the sanctity of human life:
for beneath our hysterical shouts that biological life is the
sole value, that which is to be preserved at whatever cost,
I detect a sadness born out of our memory of a better past,
out of a sense of what we have lost as a result of our long
spiritual deterioration.

If literature teaches us anything, it teaches us that there
are many things worse than dying. Think of the truly great
books you have read, and prominent among your memories
will be a series of death scenes. Recall not only Sophocles
and Shakespearè, but Prince Andrew in *War and Peace*, or
Conrad's Lord Jim or even Hemingway's Katherine Bar-
clay. Or consider what seems to me to be the counterimage
of all that we are in our lives and our art: the sequence that
describes the death of Don Quixote. As you will remember, the old knight has suffered his last and worst defeat,
under the terms of which he must give up for a whole year
his quest on behalf of his imaginary Dulcinea. So he returns home, but he is still uncured of his insanity, and his
intention is to wait out the time until he can fight again by
leading the pastoral life of a shepherd. But before this plan
can be fulfilled, Don Quixote regains his reason and grows
desperately ill.

The roles that have sustained the entire narrative are
suddenly reversed. Upon seeing the mortal danger in which
Don Quixote lies, Sancho Panza, who has been the voice of
reason, now urges that the scheme hatched in insanity be

pursued. " 'Ah, master,' cried Sancho through his tears, 'don't die, your Grace, but take my advice and go on living for many years to come; for the greatest madness that a man can be guilty of in this life is to die without good reason, without anyone's killing him, slain only by the hands of melancholy.' " Sancho is both right and wrong. Sorrow is not a sufficient reason for death, but it is we, not Don Quixote, who die of melancholy. What Don Quixote realizes at last is that neither the reality nor the value of human life is constant. If I read the book properly, one of its meanings is that all mundane existence participates in quixotic madness. Even Sancho can be seduced by totally unrealistic promises of power and riches. His reason is flawed by the pull of the here and now, of earthly desires and practical considerations. Don Quixote, standing at the edge of death, is able to see a larger truth and to put not only his own madness, but all of human life into a new perspective.

Our cause is the opposite of his, for we have abandoned all our avenues to that vision. Left with only the life of the flesh, the life of this world, we grow sadder by the day, for as I have attempted to show, existence apart from a concept of belief is unsupportable. We hate ourselves for what we have become, and under the guise of that familiar Freudian self-deception, we long for what we claim to abhor : in our despair we yearn for death. Which is to say, we want to live forever. As intellectuals and writers and increasingly as a people, we take as our single goal perpetuation of the flesh itself. With dedicated monomania, we work to increase the length of physical life, to keep the heart beating, to keep the cancer from spreading, to terminate wars, and cut down the automobile accident rate, that each of us may carry his spiritual death into centuries to come when there might even be a cure for senility.

These ambitions, laudable when pursued in the proper context, are, when they are sought in isolation, a denial of life. So the deep discontents that we suffer, the disarrangements and fragmentations of our society amply demonstate. And this is the first thing that the new breed of writer, and particularly the new breed of southern writer, must understand. The flesh without the spirit is nothing, and the search for the life of the body, unvitalized by the soul, is in the very truest sense a search for death. The young southern writer must understand this in a way that Faulkner did not have to understand it, because he must compensate for the loss of belief that has taken place in society at large. That is, he must develop in his own soul the values that he once could draw from his culture; he must now furnish for himself what every southern novelist could claim for his birthright thirty years ago. Toward this end, he must divest himself of errors of the past and present.

To begin with, the writer must reject the notion that art is god, or that the artistic practice and end deserve his first loyalty. And he will find this excruciatingly difficult to do. The craft of writing is so hard to learn, the apprenticeship is so long, the work is so arduous, and even the smallest success is born of so much suffering, the young novelist or poet will find it almost impossible not to attach first importance to his work and to think of what he does as an ultimate vocation. But he must remember that before he acts, he must be: before he finds form and method for the embodiment of his temperament which will make its appeal to the world at large, he must accept the only proper terms under which this temperament can develop. He must have a concept of self-environment for literary endeavor by integrating the finite and the infinite, the mundane and the spiritual, which is to say, he must reclaim the religious view. That this vision will not be the same in detail or dogma as that once furnished by the social ambience should go without saying. But the spiritual quality, the sense of a divine reality, must be restored by the artist if the art is to survive.

For technique, important as it is, is simply a manifestation of what the writer is able to perceive. Shakespeare is the greatest technician of our language because his understanding of the human condition was truer than that of any other English writer. Dreiser's prose was often bad because he was often wrong about life. I point this out because though the study of technical values is a legitimate and even indispensable pursuit for the writer, method is nothing without vision, and vision must come first. In other words, if it were in our power to learn to write the way Faulkner wrote—which it is not—then we should come to that knowledge by learning to think as Faulkner thought and to see as Faulkner saw, not by copying the patterns of his sentences or the structure of his books. So we turn our attention first to the sickness of the spirit, and if we are diligent and willing to make the sacrifice, we shall, by grace, come to a new view of our world.

Initially, we shall see dimly, but this much we should be able to make out. In the exacerbations and polarizations of our time, good and evil are manifesting themselves in terms at once more subtle and more flagrant than ever before. Disorder, which is a final conformation of evil, is everywhere, and we must encompass this fact in our work without either disordering the work itself or suffering an accompanying disorder of our own spirits. By this I mean that we must avoid the temptation to portray evil for its own sake, or evil unrelieved by good, or good uninformed by a sense of cosmic reality. We must see the conflicts of our age in their full significance. We must find images that will convey the full scale of the battle, and nothing less than the stake for which the struggle is being joined, which is the spiritual survival of mankind. I cannot tell you what these images will be: each person will select his own according to his temperament. But they do exist and even abound, particularly here in the South where finding the heroism in disaster and creating beauty out of ruins has become a habit. If we are good enough and lucky enough in the execution of our task, then we and those who read us will move into life once more, immune for a time at least, from death by melancholy.

# Index

131